The
Magic-Weaving Business

The
Magic-Weaving Business

---

*Finding the heart
of learning and teaching*

Sir John Jones
Foreword by Michael Fullan

LEANNTA PUBLISHING
London, United Kingdom

First published 2009
by Leannta Publishing
63 Arlington Avenue, London N1 7BA

A catalogue record for this book is available from the British Library.

ISBN 978-0-9563760-0-8

Printed and bound in UK by City Printing, London.
FIRST EDITION

To Mum and Bill
who have always been there for me
and weaved their own special magic.

Contents

Foreword

by

Michael Fullan

Sir John Jones, a bit of a magic-weaver himself, has written a wonderful odyssey of learning experiences that give us hope and reality that all children can, and do, learn when educators put their minds and hearts to it. Capturing both the struggles and the romance of educational transformation, Sir John, with a touch of curmudgeon-like impatience and plenty of humour, takes the mystery out of the business and the vocation of magic-weaving.

The stories in The Magic-Weaving Business are heart-warming and inspiring. They possess pitch-perfect balance between passion and analytical insight. Sir John starts us off with what is clearly going to be a different adventure than we have ever had before through the medium of a book. Chapter one talks about: 'understanding the magic', 'a threshold adventure', 'if the dream is big enough', 'the voice in your head', 'synchronicity', and 'to serve them all my days'. Wow!

In addition to stories of passion, integrity and wisdom, we are reminded that 'righteous indignation' is sometimes warranted. Sir John has a way of giving us ideas that 'stick' in our soul. This is a book that you will stay with you.

Each of the chapters digs deeper into the key themes introduced in chapter one as mentioned above. I especially liked the power of synchronicity in which ten powerful elements are woven together: understand and live moral purpose; all people are of equal value; teach love of history; attitude is key; children will never forget how we make them feel; learning occurs at the edge of your comfort zone; the biggest influence on another's behaviour is my behaviour; the problem is the problem not the child; those who need our support most of all probably deserve it the least; and they will be smart enough if we are good enough. Such gems.

The Magic-Weaving Business is a book of action, values and reflection driving each other. The circles of calling, synchronicity and reflection capture the whole business in three sets of overlapping virtues: passion, wisdom and righteous indignation; reflected in our beliefs, words and deeds; and deeply grounded in the person, who am I, why do I do it, and what to be.

Sir John makes education at once personal and relational—turn up, know their identity, remember them, create an 'I can' reality, and always be an actor not a reactor. This book will stay with you long after you read it. Why? Because of how it makes you feel.

Preface

Babar Ali lives in Murshidabad, West Bengal. He attends the Raj Govinda school which is 10km away. Every day he catches an auto-rickshaw part of the way and walks the rest. Babar Ali is the first person in his family to go to school. He is 16 years old.

At 14, Chumki Hajra has never been to school. Instead she washes dishes and cleans houses for 200 rupees (£3) a month. If she does not work, her family will not survive. But now Chumki can go to school.

When he gets home at four o'clock each day, Babar Ali rings a bell. At first they came in a trickle, but now 800 children from poor families line up in the yard behind his house, for lessons from Babar Ali and ten friends from his school. After singing the national anthem, the students get down to their studies. There is no charge and no trouble. Between her shifts, squeezed on a rough wooden bench with 12 others, by the light of two bulbs (when the electricity holds), Chumki scribbles her notes and dreams of being a nurse.

Babar Ali is called the youngest headteacher in the world. He knows that without an education these children stand little chance. Babar Ali is a weaver of magic.

In some of the world's poorest countries, having a good education is more important than putting food on the table. Why is it that, in some areas of the so-called developed world, there is a declining respect for teachers and, paradoxically, in many of the poorest parts, a lack of belief in the value of education?

This book is my humble attempt at suggesting how we might reach out to every learner. It is the first part of a trilogy; it deals with the teacher's role. The series will later explore how school leaders and systems leaders may help.

Magic-weaving is not new. From Socrates to Senge, from Confucius to Capello, from Mandela to Mother Teresa, great teachers have made the difference by touching lives, pushing back the boundaries and making the seemingly impossible possible. Such magic often goes unappreciated but is indelibly etched on the hearts of those who experience it.

My work has led me to a point where literally thousands of people have described their school experience as pivotal to their development and the influence of a teacher as crucial to their success. We never forget that great teacher; the one who took us to places where we could not go alone; the one we came back to visit all those years later; the ones who changed our lives by opening doors for us. It might have been a coach, a mentor, a friend, the biology teacher or your mum and dad.

For Chumki Hajra it is Babar Ali.

Magic weavers are all around us.

This book tells their story.

Chapter One

Understanding the magic

In search of magic • The power of righteous indignation • Tackling social injustice

In search of magic

The National Commission on Teaching and America's Future (NCTAF) was convened in 1994.[1] The commission's title itself defined its purpose; central to its brief was an exploration of the power of teaching. Many people were called to give witness to a bold hypothesis that schooling, in general, and teaching, in particular, could impact significantly on the life chances of those who experience them.

> Have you ever had a teacher, one who saw you as a raw but precious thing, a jewel that with care could be polished to a fine stone?
>
> If you are ever lucky enough to find your way to such a teacher, you will always find your way back.

As part of the evidence submitted to the commission, a young teacher sat, nervously, before this august body and spoke these powerful words:[2]

> *I was supposed to be a welfare statistic…It is because of a teacher that I sit at this table. I remember her telling us one cold miserable day that she could not make our clothing better; she could not provide us with food; she could not change the terrible segregated conditions under which we lived. She could introduce us to the world of reading, the world of books, and that is what she did.*

Then the young teacher closed her eyes and spoke wistfully.

> *What a world! I visited Asia and Africa. I saw magnificent sunsets; I tasted exotic foods. I fell in love and danced in wonderful halls. I ran away with escaped slaves and stood beside a teenage martyred saint. I visited lakes and streams and composed lines of verse. I knew then that I wanted to help children do the same things. I wanted to weave magic…*

Evelyn Jenkins Gunn

So if you are involved in any way in developing the potential of young people, as teacher, coach, mentor or parent, when someone asks you what you do for a living be bold and say, " I'm in the magic-weaving business!" … and they'll probably move away.

During a recent presentation, I invited the audience to think back to their schooldays and try to recall a teacher who had made a difference to them; who had a positive impact on their life; someone who had weaved a little magic. After asking the delegates to exchange their memories of that person with a neighbour, I wondered if any of them would like to share their recollection with the whole group, some 400 people. A young woman, in her first year of teaching, nervously raised her hand.

"I would like to tell you about my magic-weaver. I always remember her with a smile on her face. We called it *that smile*; it warmed you. She was always at the door to greet you. Not only did she know your name, she knew your identity. She always remembered our birthdays. She had that knack of making you feel good about yourself. As a teenager, I lost my confidence and self-belief for a period and she told me not to worry, that she would look after them for me until I was ready to take them back. We joked about her being the keeper of dreams but I guess that's exactly what she was. My mother died when I was at school and on the first anniversary of her death this teacher was the one who put her arm around me in the playground and whispered, 'Are you OK today? I'm here if you need me.' She was the oasis in my desert and she is the reason I became a teacher."

The audience sat stunned and silent. "Where is she now?" I asked.

The young teacher raised her hand and, pointing across the room, answered my question. "She's sitting right over there." And bowing her head respectfully towards her old teacher she whispered, "Thank you."

Four hundred delegates burst into spontaneous applause and cheering which continued for several minutes. Everyone was smiling except the young teacher and her older mentor who were both crying. But these were not tears of sorrow.

It struck me how lucky the older teacher was to be given the opportunity to have her magic-weaving so publicly acknowledged. Most will never be so fortunate. The Chinese, as always, have an old saying which states that you can measure the quality of a culture when old people are prepared to plant seeds that will grow into trees under whose shade they will never sit. This notion of selfless, often unrecognised, service is the reality for many teachers, yet still they answer the call.

In the past four years, I have had the opportunity to present numerous workshops and training programmes both in the UK and abroad. I have worked with about 35,000 colleagues from: primary schools, special schools, pupil referral units, secondary schools and FE colleges. I have presented to, and exchanged ideas with, more than 10,000 headteachers, school principals and their deputies.

It has been my privilege to spend time in the company of magic-weavers who have willingly shared their knowledge and expertise. Along the way, I have used my time to collect, collate and categorise nuggets of good learning. As a result, I have been able to assemble a database of great ideas and strategies that work.

I do not take the credit for them; they are not mine. But what they represent is a rich vein of talent and professional ability, resident in many.

This book tells the story.

Most magic-weavers admit that they are not born with these skills, but they learn them through reading, watching others, listening, talking and practising. The good news is that it is possible for all of us to learn and practise such skills. For some people they come easily; the rest of us need to recognise, understand, practise and internalise these ideas until they become second nature. They are simple actions accrued through years of hard experience and, if carried out systematically and consistently, they actually work.

A teacher once described how he had bumped into dozens of past students and not one of them had ever said, "Hey sir, that worksheet changed my life!"

"And I spent hours on those worksheets," he bemoaned

Some jobs have clearly defined outcomes. There is a tangible pay-off or product: a brand new car at the end of an assembly line or a patient fully recovered after a complex operation. While good marks in a difficult examination will give both the student and teacher great satisfaction, countless teachers have confirmed to me that this is only part of the story. (Data analysts please take note). Schools are preparing students not just to pass examinations; there is much more to it than that. They are preparing them for life.

As we grow older we realise that much of what we learned in school is forgotten in time, unless we teach it. If you doubt this, have a look at the old examination papers you sat. How well would you do now? My experience with magic-weavers has confirmed my belief in the old maxim that children will forget what teachers made them think but will never forget how they made them feel. For school, like life, is building powerful, lasting memories.

In a moving speech, I once heard Mick Waters describe how children carry messages to a time and place we will never see.[3] The greater pleasure lies, teachers constantly remind me, not just in the content of the curriculum, nor in examination success, but also in the other messages that children carry. In this book, I want to explore those memories, those messages.

During a coffee break at a conference in southern England, I was approached by a man who, though not part of the audience that day, had attended my presentation a year earlier. He reminded me that in the session, I had engaged the audience in an exercise of remembering their magic-weaver at school. I had made them promise that they would try to find that person and thank them. He explained how it had taken him some months to trace the teacher who had taught him when he was eleven-years old.

Eventually he had found the man, now well into his nineties. He managed to obtain an email address and felt somewhat apprehensive that, after all this time, the old man might have no idea who he was. Nevertheless, he started to type:

You will probably not remember me, but you taught me many years ago. At a recent conference I attended, the speaker asked us to remember a teacher who had been an inspiration, someone who had made a difference. I immediately thought of you and felt that after all these years it was about time I contacted you to say thank you.

He had, he admitted, pressed the 'Send' button with a little trepidation and no real hope of a reply. But not long after he sent the message, his 'Notice of mail' bleeped and, with a mixture of disbelief and excitement, he pressed 'Open'.

'Of course I remember you Smithy,' it read. 'In fact I am attaching a photograph of our infamous trip to Scarborough. You will remember it well. It rained every day and it was freezing. That's you, third from the left on the back row. I can still see your little knees knocking together in the cold and your bottom lip quivering in the wind, but you never complained once. Of course I remember you. Thank you so much for remembering me.'

However, that was not the end of the story.

A few days later the wife of the old teacher rang my colleague to tell him that her husband had died the day before. But, she continued, "this is not a sad phone call because, for the last few days of his life, all he had talked about was that lovely school, the joy of teaching and a little boy called Smithy. Thank you so much," she concluded, "you got there just in time."

The power of righteous indignation

A hundred years from now, it will not matter what kind of house we lived in, what kind of car we drove, or what our bank account balance was. But the world may be different because we made a difference in the life of a child.

Everyone chooses their own attitude in life. People may try to influence your attitude and sometimes they succeed, but only if you let them. Victor Frankl tells us that choosing our own attitude is our ultimate freedom.

During the Korean War, more American soldiers died in captivity than in any conflict before that. It was not physical but psychological torture that caused their deaths. The torturers skilfully and systematically removed all hope from these young troops that they would ever be free and allowed to go home. As a result, 30% of these young men crawled into the corner of their cell and died, devoid of hope, their capacity to set themselves goals and dream of freedom terminally damaged. Their life ceased to have a meaning.

Statistics show that those men and women who retire without any clear notion of what they wish to achieve in their retirement have a shorter life expectancy than those who are able to identify new goals and horizons. Scratch any happy person and you will find a project.

We all need a sense of purpose and direction. Human beings are teleological. Teleology, the theory that there is a purpose to existence and that order in the universe is not random, means that we are, by nature, goal-setters and goal-seekers. Goal-setting is simply putting pictures into our minds towards which we can move. Guided missiles are teleological and work in similar ways. Human beings without goals become aimless drifters, lost in a sea of uncertainty and hostage to the latest fad or fashion.

In his book *Man's Search for Meaning*, Victor Frankl describes life in the Nazi concentration camps.[4] He describes how those who had goals, thinking beyond the horror of the day-to-day reality, had a better chance of survival than those who dwelled on the daily horror and gave up hope.

So having a purpose is vital to our well-being and most writers on change seem to agree that, for individuals or whole organisations, a strong sense of purpose and direction, a 'beginning with the end in mind,' (Covey)[5] or a moral purpose (Fullan)[6] is essential for personal growth or organisational success.

At conferences, I ask those who work with young people to consider their moral purpose or, more simply, why they do what they do. The responses from delegates tend to fall into three categories.

- A minority see teaching merely as a job.
- A second group regards it as a career.
- A third group, the largest, describes it as a calling.[7]

Curiously, though not in every case, the way individuals see their role can be linked, I think, to the degree of commitment made to what they do.

Different people connect at different levels. Louise Stoll sees 'connectedness' as three-dimensional:[8] physical, intellectual and emotional. I found, through discussion, that there appears to be a link between: how people see the role they play, the degree of commitment they are prepared to make and the level of connectedness with which they feel comfortable.

As a headteacher (school principal) I was always saddened and frustrated by those who saw teaching as just another job. Yes, they physically connected. They turned up, put in the time, earned their money and returned home. Inevitably, they complained about: the attitude of the students, excess workload, meetings running over time, long parents' evenings, and any other activity which seemed to stray outside their contractual commitment.

Hemingway described such people as 'bankrupt of spirit'.[9] In his novel *The Sun Also Rises*, Brett asks Jake Barnes how he became bankrupt. He replies that it was gradually to begin with and then it came suddenly. And in a way that is how it happens. The fire simply goes out, slowly and relentlessly. They turn up and they connect, but only physically. They lose their passion and purpose; teaching becomes a series of tedious tasks to be undertaken until the last bell sounds.

"They've retired," one delegate observed, "they just haven't bothered to tell the principal yet."

Often the first to notice this are the children. In a primary classroom, a visitor asked a young boy the name of his teacher.

"The terminator," the boy replied. The visitor looked puzzled. "So many children, so little time," he explained. And he was right. She was terrifying; but it was the deadness in her eyes that disturbed the visitor most.

When I was headteacher I made no secret of my dislike for interviewing staff. The artificiality of the question and response process, I felt, at best, gave us only the opportunity to connect cognitively with interviewees and discover 'what' they were. I preferred to have coffee privately with each candidate and endeavour to discover 'who' they were. I had only one question in my head and that was 'Would I want any of my own children to spend any time in the company of this person?'

I became relatively adept at what Malcolm Gladwell described as 'thin-slicing' in his book *Blink*.[10] That ability to make quick judgements about people. I was not looking for someone who would just turn up, who would give me their physical commitment. I wanted a lot more. And so did the students.

The second group seems more drawn to teaching as a career. They are ambitious, keen to do well, impress and progress. As with the first group, they connect physically. But I also find that such individuals, while they enjoy teaching, tend to connect cognitively, through the power of their ideas. In my experience more secondary than primary teachers fall into this category. Perhaps this is not surprising given that there are more opportunities for career progression in secondary schools and more of an emphasis on subjects and curriculum content. Someone once said, rather mischievously, that primary teachers tend to love the children, secondary teachers love their subjects and university teachers love themselves. My research, albeit not statistically rigorous, would tend to support the first two claims. Far be it from me to support the third.

My frustration with much of the training and development of teachers is that it often requires and, to some extent encourages, participants to engage cognitively with activity; stimulated intellectually but unmoved emotionally. It is no surprise that nothing has been so frustrating as the thousands of hours of professional development undertaken by teachers which resulted in no change in behaviour once they returned to their classrooms.[11]

The third group describe their role as a calling. I wasn't sure initially what that meant except that implicit to its meaning is an emotional as well as an intellectual and physical commitment to the role. When I ask members of this group to describe why they became a teacher the phrase which crops up again and again is: 'I wanted to make a difference'.

Within my search for a meaning, I ask delegates to recall their magic-weaver or someone of such quality with whom they work or have worked. Long lists of characteristics emerge and I have identified three key, generic, characteristics of such individuals which enable them to make this difference. Words such as: 'enthusiastic', 'love of the job', 'fire in the belly', 'eccentric', 'passionate', 'ardent' and 'emotional' made it relatively easy to identify the first key characteristic of such people. They have *passion*. What the Spanish call *'ganas'*.

They embody a commitment to their higher purpose of making a difference so that, even in moments of self-doubt, they seem able to sustain themselves with its power. They commit themselves not just physically and intellectually but emotionally too. William Murray described the force that real commitment creates in his book *The Scottish Himalayan Expedition.*[12]

Near the beginning of the book, Murray refers to the limited preparations that were made for the expedition, with one vital exception. They had committed themselves to the expedition and this in itself put them half way there in their minds. He reflects that until that moment, there is always the possibility to hesitate and give up.[13] The reason many great initiatives and creative endeavours fail is through lack of commitment. The moment you commit yourself, it is almost like providence moves with you.

From that moment on, things happen to help you that you never expected. Once you make your decision and act in a certain way, it leads to other unforeseen events, meetings and all kinds of material assistance that come your way that you would never have predicted or even dreamed about.

According to the dictionary, passion is 'intense emotion'.

While it is sometimes difficult to detect, it is not so hard to spot its absence.

Passion is one of life's essential elements.

If you put your heart, mind and soul into whatever you do, you give it more meaning.

Passion will give you the strength to succeed, no matter what you face in life. Nothing can take its place and nothing will be achieved without it.

Passion is all powerful.

Once they made their emotional commitment to go, the material resources followed naturally.

But it is not just passion alone that marks out such individuals. Another generic list of words emerges: 'caring', 'kind', 'fair', 'just', 'thoughtful', 'helpful', 'considerate' and 'compassionate'. Such individuals seem to possess a *wisdom* which has less to do with cognitive sharpness and intellectual capacity and more to do with what one of them called 'people savvy' or what Daniel Goleman calls emotional intelligence. That is the capacity to understand and manage emotions, both our own and those of others; the ability to build and sustain relationships and the key skill of empathy.[14]

At the second school where I was headteacher, we invited students to choose their own mentor. Acknowledging that the system allocated them with teachers, tutors and pastoral carers, we thought they should have the opportunity to pick someone with whom they could connect. Put simply, someone they rated and liked. It was always a relief to have someone select you. Sadly some staff had no-one pick them. The person who was chosen by more students than any other qualified staff member was Joan Bennett. Joan was a cleaner. But Joan had this … this magic. "When I'm with Joan," one student explained, "I feel good about myself."

Passion and wisdom are essential to magic-weaving, but there is a third quality which characterises this group. Words and phrases such as: 'strong sense of commitment', 'moral purpose', 'drive', 'mission', 'every child matters', 'of equal worth', 'dedicated', and 'no child left behind', appeared regularly on conference flipcharts. And I struggled to find a generic word or phrase which caught the essence of what they were trying to express.

Goleman's model of emotional intelligence has four constructs:
1. Self-awareness
2. Self-management
3. Social awareness
4. Relationship management

Goleman develops a range of emotional competencies within each construct. He considers them as learned capabilities that we can all develop, in time.

Some weeks before Barack Obama was elected President of the United States, I was sitting in a diner in Tucson, Arizona where I was attending a conference about *The Kids Left Behind* with some magic-weavers from the UK.[15] I wrote 'The Calling' at the centre of a Venn diagram (Model A). In two of the three conjoining circles I pencilled in 'Passion' and 'Wisdom'. It was the third, still blank, circle which continued to trouble me - the third key characteristic of those magic-weavers who answered the call.

Christine Yorston[16], who works in the London borough of Hackney, asked me what I was doing. I described the origins of the diagram and my difficulty finding a name for the third circle.

"That's easy," she offered, without hesitation, "it's righteous indignation. That's what should burn within all of us, but particularly in a teacher."

Later that day I showed the diagram to a fellow delegate at the conference from North Carolina. "What do you think?" I asked. "She's absolutely right," she replied without hesitation. "It is righteous indignation that will get Obama to the White House. A burning, simmering sense of frustration, anger even, at the injustice and unfairness of life. He is living proof that, given the right opportunities and a good education, everyone can succeed and no one will be left behind.

"How strange that just four decades ago when Governor Wallace gave his infamous 'Segregation Now ... Segregation Forever' speech, thousands of people marched the streets of Alabama just for the RIGHT to vote.[17] They were beaten, spat upon and abused. But it was righteous indignation that gave them courage to ride the buses and walk the streets.

"Rosa Parkes sat on that bus so that Martin Luther King could stand on that platform. And Martin Luther King stood on that platform so that Barack Obama could run for President. And Barack Obama is running for President so that we can all be free. It's a great story. I wonder if North Carolina will vote Democrat?" she mused.

Ten days later Obama won. And North Carolina did!

"I have a dream that one day, down in Alabama, with its vicious racists, with its governor having his lips dripping with words of 'interposition' and 'nullification' – one day right there in Alabama little black boys and black girls will be able to join hands with little white boys and white girls as sisters and brothers."

Martin Luther King

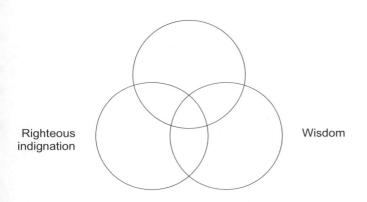

Passion

Righteous indignation

Wisdom

Model A: The Calling

This diagram represents all the characteristics identified by colleagues while thinking about magic-weavers who had made a difference to them.

The stories and statistics I will share not only reinforce the power of the teacher's role but also underline the responsibility the profession has to understand what Michael Fullan describes as its moral purpose. I am going to go in search of that purpose; to understand its magic; to explore its power; to measure its effects; to confirm it is learnable and not confined to a few naturals; to test my belief that to teach is one of the best yet toughest calls anyone can answer. You cannot, I suggest, have best without toughest.

As I sat thin-slicing candidates, I knew that if I could find someone who would connect physically, cognitively and emotionally, and if I could detect passion, wisdom and righteous indignation, I would be appointing someone who would be unstoppable. Someone who could weave magic in the lives of young people.

As I collated the evidence of my research, I began to map out what it was that set such people apart. They know, in answering the call, that they can make a difference in the lives of young people by combining: passion, wisdom and righteous indignation. But there was more. There appeared to be another combination present. Not one key feature, a particular style or simply a random combination of behaviours that weaved the magic, but a powerful synchronicity in three things:

Tackling social injustice

- what they *believe* and *value*
- what they *say*
- what they *do.*

Most people believe that all children can learn. Many people will tell you that's the case. Judge them by what they do about it.

Simple patterns of human behaviour delivered with a consistency and synchronicity which yield great power and influence.

Mahatma Ghandi claimed that true happiness lay in the harmony between what you think, what you say, and what you do. Perhaps what Carl Rogers called a 'way of being' or what David Bouchard, the children's author, in a speech I heard him deliver in Toronto, described as the power of modelling.[18] It was, Bouchard claimed, not *a* way to influence and change others but *the* way. If parents believe in the power of reading, talk passionately about it to their children and are voracious readers themselves then their children will probably learn and love to read.

Doing things by example is not just the best way to influence others; it's the only way that works.

"You are somebody's hero," Bouchard challenged the parents in the audience, "so step up to the plate or get off the team."

Initially, I described this combination as a kind of personal integrity; the core or moral purpose of an individual (their beliefs and values) being reflected in what you see (their behaviour) and resonant in what you hear (their words).

But integrity is an elusive concept. Many have gone in search of this elusiveness; my favourite definition stating that integrity is simply what you do when no-one else is watching. The simple, yet potent, ability to *walk the talk*. But any discussion on integrity is inevitably value-ridden, laced with morality and a sense of what is right and what is wrong.

Adolf Hitler yielded power and influence from a combination of his words, deeds and beliefs, however misguided, distorted or erroneous. Today, Osama Bin Laden may do the same; his global influence is almost immeasurable. But men of integrity? That's a difficult concept to imagine. Yet the powerful combination of their beliefs, values, words and deeds gave and gives them tremendous influence over millions of people.

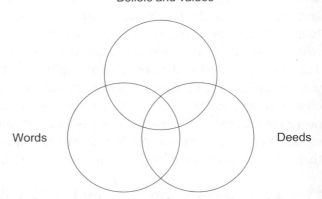

Beliefs and values

Words

Deeds

Model B: Circles of Synchronicity

It is not their integrity but their synchronicity that is the source of their power. When what I believe in and value is consistently evident in what I say and do, while you may not agree with or espouse the same world view, there exists an undoubted force which is difficult to resist. It is in the combination of all three attributes that the alchemy lies. I call this force the 'Circles of Synchronicity' (Model B).

When there is dissonance in the three, individuals appear dishonest, organisations seem flawed and systems weak. On an individual level, magic-weavers seem to create harmony between the three. I explore examples of such synchronicity in Chapter Five. What is undoubted is their ability, learned or instinctive, to harness the power of synchronicity.

I have visited many schools where the mission statement preaches equality. Then I watch staff walk straight to the front of lunch queues or discover that non-teaching staff are not welcome into staffrooms. Or schools where the fulfilling of the potential of each individual is the mission, but the students are grouped not by ability and potential but by behaviour and attitude. Where caring for each pupil is central to the school philosophy, but the students' toilets are dirty and intimidating, while those for the staff are five-star. Where pride in the students is maintained, but the students are not allowed to walk across the school foyer for fear of upsetting any visitors. Where the power of student voice is valued, but only a small percentage of talking in lessons is actually done by them, or they are not trusted to take part in staff appointments. Such dissonance is often striking to the onlooker but dangerously invisible to the practitioner.

There has, I fear, been a similar trend in the world of education. In an age dominated by an obsessive focus on attainment data and pupils' progress in cognitive abilities; it is easy to forget why many choose to be a teacher and what parents want from school for their children. The development of literate, numerate young people, with a relatively broad knowledge of the world around them, is important but this is only part of the jigsaw. Across the world I have asked parents what they want from school for their children. Their priorities are strongly consistent: first they want their children to be happy, second they want them to be safe and third they would like them to achieve something, *in that order*. When teachers talk of making a difference they are not talking just about the school's position in the performance league table.

There is so much more to schooling than the slavish adherence to data analysis and test results. But in the eighties, we tilted headlong into an age of public accountability with a series of education acts heralding the arrival of Ofsted, league tables, national testing and all the paraphernalia of naming and shaming. Our young people became the most tested group of youngsters on the planet and our teachers, arguably, the most inspected. The *we shall leave no child untested* strategy.

Andy Hargreaves outlines graphically the effects of such strategies in the USA and England:[19]

> *A high stakes literacy test that was linked to graduation and whose results were made public drove schools towards cynical solutions – narrowing the curriculum, teaching to the test and concentrating excessive attention on coaching children just below the cut-off point. In the United States and England, the effects of these standardised testing regimes were even worse – schools rejected children who might bring the scores down, new entrants were were given no attention if their results didn't count that year, or test items were made progressively easier to fabricate political*

appearances of improvement. Cheating
spread like wildfire. Corruption was rife.

I have nothing against accountability but believe that the introduction of such measures should have been preceded by a national debate on the core values and the moral purpose of education. This would have created the values-words-actions synchronicity lacking in national policy at the time.

Policy documents such as *Excellence and Enjoyment*[20] (not *or* enjoyment) and *Every Child Matters*[21] re-engaged professionals in the debate we should have had in the eighties. Put simply – are we preparing children for examinations or for life? Is it the test result slip or the kind of human beings we produce at the end of their time in school that matters? Is it time to reconsider the real purpose of education? I sense a real feeling of frustration around the country from the professionals in schools that for too long the assessment tail has wagged the education dog and that education is in danger of losing its soul. Lord David Putnam outlined the challenge in a speech in Birmingham.[22] "It is time," he said, "to wrestle the assessment beast to the ground."

The consequences of not doing so are subtle and worrying. I was in a primary classroom and pointed to a child, wanting to know her name. The teacher assumed otherwise and said, "She's a level 3a." In discussion with that teacher, who was very good at her job, she readily admitted that it was sometimes difficult not to see a child but a national curriculum level.

Gary Wilson described to me how he stood outside a room in which some primary school children were sitting a national test (SAT) for creative writing.

"How did you do?" Gary asked a boy leaving the room.

"I got two semi-colons in!" the boy proudly announced.

Later Gary asked the group, "Why do we write?" "To get a level 4," they replied, without hesitation.

Too much is at stake to get it wrong. The Organisation for Economic Co-operation and Development (OECD) is clear about the power of education stating that schooling is the 'central socialising point, at a neighbourhood level, for the regeneration of our communities.'[23] If demographics is not to determine destiny (Barr and Parrett, see note[14]) then we have to restore the balance between the value of raised attainment levels and the importance of the development of the whole child.

When he was schools standards minister, David Miliband took the opportunity to remind us all that education is still the most effective weapon available to break the link between where a person is born and how well they do in life.[24]

And how does that life begin? In the developed world life starts rather inauspiciously for most of us, in a plastic manger in the local maternity unit with a great deal of noise at one end and a total lack of responsibility at the other. It is at this moment that the lottery called life begins to take effect. The baby is taken away by someone to a life it does not choose. What if the baby could choose? "Look," it would plead, "a four-bedroomed, detached house in a nice part of town. Cobble driveway, Porsche Carrera parked up front, wrong colour but I'll cope."

"Oh no," say the parents, "we live down here…"
So the lottery of life is played out and, as with all
lotteries, some win but many lose. Life is not fair.
Does the environment to which we are taken have an
effect? Common sense would suggest so but can
research support the idea?

Research by Leon Feinstein from Institute of
Education, London, suggests that family income does
affect how well you do.[25] Using data from children
born in 1970, he compared children from different
socio-economic backgrounds and how they performed
relatively from 22 months old to the age of ten. The
solid blue lines show the progress of children from
high socio-economic status while the black dashed
lines represent the progress of children from low
socio-economic status.

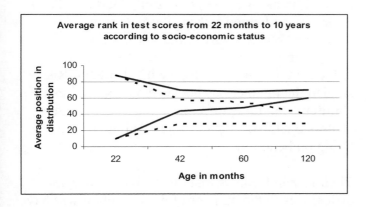

Compare the progress of children from poor
backgrounds (black dashed line) ranked in the top
10% at age 22 months, with that of children from
affluent families (blue solid line) ranked in the lowest
10% at age 22 months. The lower-ability, rich kids
overtake the smarter, poor kids between ages six and
seven; the gap widens from then on.

You may be thinking that was children born in 1970,
things are much better now, especially with recent

government investments in education and childcare. If so, then you would be wrong. Jo Blanden and Stephen Machin replicated the research with the millennium cohort (born in 2000-2001) and found exactly the same pattern in their data between the ages of three and five years.[26]

The Independent Commission on Social Mobility reported in 2009 that a child's chances of success in the UK still depend largely on the background and earnings of his or her parents.[27] While this depressing report suggests that nothing much has changed in recent years, it remains too simplistic to assume that wealth itself is the reason for this disparity in educational progress. So, what actually makes the difference?

Ground-breaking research by Betty Hart and Todd Risley in the United States pinpoints some significant reasons why children from poor backgrounds fall behind those from richer families in their intellectual development.[28] Hart and Risley studied the interactions between parents and their children from three different family backgrounds: professional, working class and welfare (those living on benefits).

Their research shows that by the age of four, the differences in the number of words a child will have addressed to it are staggering:

- Professional family   50 million
- Working class family   30 million
- Family on benefits   12 million

The environment in which we spend our early years is significant in terms of our literacy development. A mistake we sometimes make in schools at this stage is that we confuse the gap between 50 million and 12 million with ability. It has nothing to do with ability. There are as many gifted and talented children in the 12 million word group as there are in the 50 million word group, they were just taken to another address from that maternity unit.

But there is not just a literacy deficit to be overcome there is an emotional one, too. For it is not only the number of words experienced, it is also the quality of these words that has a significant effect. If, on a pan scale, they are divided into words of encouragement on the one side, and discouragement on the other, the discrepancy is disturbing. Once again, analysed according to family background: professional (P), working-class (W), on benefits (B). This time, the number of encouragements and discouragements, or prohibitions, each year:

Family	Encouragement	Discouragement
• P	166,000	26,000
• W	62,000	36,000
• B	26,000	57,000

The work of Barbara Fredrickson described the effect of positivity and negativity ratios, the power of positive or negative interactions, on the development of self-esteem, self-confidence and well-being in individuals.[29] The ratio of positive to negative is vital. Some children arrive in schools with odds stacked against them while others enjoy the tremendous benefits their socio-economic status hands them. Life is not fair.

While school is the first real experience of failure for many children it draws our attention to these differences, to the lottery.[30] Schools tend to label the differences or grade them. If you were not aware of the differences before, you certainly are once you take your first step through the door of a school.

I do not wish to imply blame in presenting these statistics. The fault cannot be laid at the parents' door for many of them had the same challenges to overcome, the same barriers to confront, as they themselves struggled with the cycle of deprivation. It is simply a place to begin the magic-weaving.

But in the face of so many challenges and barriers to success in life, can educators possibly make a difference to the life chances of young people? The barriers, clearly, are numerous, well-documented and daunting[31].

Comparisons of social mobility in countries across Europe and North America show that it is roughly the same in UK and USA but significantly lower than in Canada and the Nordic countries.[32] Part of the reason for this is linked to the increasing relationship between family income and educational attainment.

Some researchers identified four key factors which influence success in life. Three of the factors: poverty, family and neighbourhood were fairly predictable. So much so that I was reminded of the scene in *Fawlty Towers* in which John Cleese (Basil), pretending to be the presenter of the quiz show *Mastermind*, rather sarcastically introduced his wife (Cybil):

"And here is our next contestant, Cybil Fawlty; specialist subject: *The bleedin' obvious*."

What is a surprise is the fourth factor, the quality of schooling. If this does not quite fall into the category of the *bleedin' obvious* then the final claim of the research certainly does; that, of the four factors, the quality of schooling, if we get it right, can be 20 times more significant than the other three.[33]

The core of quality schooling, I would argue, is not a government edict or a national policy document, but a crucial relationship between two human beings: the teacher and the student.

When I ask colleagues to write down the names of three people who were a powerful, positive influence in their life there is almost always a teacher.

However, when I ask them to write down the names of three people who were a damaging influence there is usually a teacher there, too. This is a powerful role and one whose power should never be underestimated.

It is not just teaching that exerts a powerful influence over the life chances of young people but *quality* teaching. For the latter, like parenting, can be potent yet potentially toxic; powerfully good or enduringly harmful. Haim Ginott captures this duality beautifully in a haunting piece.[34]

Ginott reaches the frightening conclusion that he, as the teacher, is the decisive element in the classroom. His approach creates the climate and his mood affects the weather. He is acutely conscious of his power to make each child's life joyful or miserable. He may inspire his class and he may torture them. He can humiliate or humour, hurt or heal.

> The good news is – schooling and teachers make the difference.
>
> The bad news is – schooling and teachers make the difference.

Through his response, he decides whether a crisis is escalated or defused and whether children are humanised or dehumanised.

The power of education should not be underestimated. World leaders know its power. Tony Blair won three elections on three issues: education, education and education. Bill Clinton, in his presidential inauguration speech, placed education and learning at the centre of his priorities. Nelson Mandela, in typically poetic style, confirms its power:[35]

> *Education is a powerful engine for personal development. It is through education that the daughter of a peasant can become a doctor, that the son of a mine-worker can become manager of the mine, and that the child of farm-workers can become president of a proud nation.*

Magic-weaving indeed!

References and notes for Chapter 1

[1] www.nctaf.org The mission of the commission is to provide an action agenda for meeting America's educational challenges, connecting the quest for higher student achievement with the need for teachers who are knowledgeable, skillful, and committed to meeting the needs of all students. The commission is dedicated to helping develop policies and practices aimed at ensuring powerful teaching and learning in all communities as America's schools and children enter the 21st century.

[2] National Commission on Teaching and America's Future (1996), *What Matters Most: Teaching for America's Future*. New York: NCTAF

[3] At the time, Mick Waters was working for the Qualifications and Curriculum Authority in England. He was responsible for reviewing the national curriculum at key stage 3, for students aged 11–14.

[4] Internationally renowned psychiatrist Victor E. Frankl endured years of unspeakable horror in Nazi death camps. During, and partly because of his suffering, Dr Frankl developed a revolutionary approach to psychotherapy known as logotherapy. At the core of his theory is the belief that man's primary motivational force is his search for meaning. His experiences and description of logotherapy are included in *Man's Search for Meaning*, first published in 1946, reprinted many times since, including 1985 New York: Washington Square Press

[5] Covey, Stephen R. (1989), *7 Habits of Highly Effective People*. London: Simon & Shuster

[6] Fullan, Michael (2003), *The Moral Imperative of School Leadership*. Thousand Oaks, CA: Corwin

[7] Metcalf, Andrew & Game, Ann (2006) *Teachers Who Change Lives*. Carlton, Victoria: Melbourne University Press. The book concerns outstanding teachers and the qualities that enable them to help change students lives for the better. The book is based on interviews with prominent Australians talking about teachers who helped shape them, and on interviews with teachers well known for their excellence.

[8] Stoll, Louise (1999), Realising Our Potential: Understanding and Developing Capacity for Lasting Improvement, in *School Effectiveness and School Improvement: An International Journal of Research, Policy and Practice* Vol 10, 4, pp 503–532

[9] *The Sun Also Rises* first appeared in 1926. It was Ernest Hemingway's first big novel and established him as one of the pre-eminent writers of his time. It encapsulates the angst of the post-World War I generation, known as the Lost Generation.

[10] Gladwell, Malcolm (2005), *Blink*. New York: Little, Brown & Co. This is a book about rapid cognition, the kind of thinking that happens in the blink of an eye. When you meet someone for the first time, your mind takes about two seconds to jump to a series of conclusions. *Blink* is about those two seconds.

[11] Joyce, Bruce R. & Showers, Beverly (2002), Integrating staff development and school improvement: A study of teacher personality and school climate. In: *Changing School Culture Through Staff Development,* pp 41–47. Alexandria, VA: Association for Supervision and Curriculum Development. Researchers Joyce and Showers show that while the study of theory, demonstrations and supported practice provide teachers with knowledge and skills, they only amount to about 5% change in actual classroom practice. With the addition of peer coaching, 95% of teachers will be able to transfer training effectively to their classrooms.

[12] Murray, William H. (1951), *The Scottish Himalayan Expedition.* London: J.M. Dent & Sons. During World War II, Murray spent three years in prisoner of war camps where he wrote his first book *Mountaineering in Scotland* on toilet paper. The manuscript was found and destroyed by the Gestapo, yet despite this loss, he started again. It was eventually published in 1947 and remains the classic text for anyone contemplating Scottish winter climbing.

[13] Murray paraphrases a famous quote from Goethe about commitment. The quote varies in translation but here is a link to the English version that Murray used: www.goethesociety.org/pages/quotescom.html

[14] Goleman, Daniel (1995), *Emotional Intelligence.* New York: Bantam. Goleman provides new ways to understand people's behaviour, attitudes and interpersonal skills.

[15] Barr, Robert D. & Parrett, William H. (2007), *The Kids Left Behind: Catching Up the Underachieving Children of Poverty.* Bloomington, IN: Solution Tree. This remarkable book synthesises best practices from the most recent research across the US into high performing, high poverty schools. It is a compelling, powerful and clear call for action to address poverty through transforming schooling.

[16] Christine Yorston is a principal primary adviser (and magic-weaver) for The Learning Trust. www.learningtrust.co.uk

[17] George Wallace was elected as Governor of Alabama in 1963. In his inaugural address he challenged the attempts by the federal government to enforce laws prohibiting segregation in Alabama's schools and colleges. Many years later, Wallace apologised for his racist views and actions. (www.archives.state.al.us/govs_list/InauguralSpeech.html) Martin Luther King responded to Wallace in his famous 'I have a dream' speech.

[18] Former teacher and principal David Bouchard is now a celebrated author of children's books and workshop presenter. David understands how children learn to read and he shares that information with passion. He is North America's foremost champion for literacy. Find out more about David's books at: www.davidbouchard.com

[19] Hargreaves, Andy (2007), The Long and Short of Educational Change. In *Education Canada*, vol. 47, no.3, p.16

[20] *Excellence and enjoyment: A strategy for primary schools* was published by the government Department for Education and Skills in 2003. It set out the future vision for primary education

that built on what had already been achieved through the national strategies. You may download the document from this website: www.nationalstrategies.standards.dcsf.gov.uk/node/85063

[21] *Every Child Matters* was the title of a government green paper published in 2003. The Children Act 2004 was built on these proposals. Since then *Every Child Matters* has developed into a slogan for a shared programme of change to improve outcomes for all children and young people in England. You may explore the different strands of the programme at this website: www.dcsf.gov.uk/everychildmatters/

[22] Lord Puttnam initiated the teachers' awards ceremony in the UK. He has a passionate interest in education following his success in the film industry. You can watch a interview of Lord Puttnam by the late Ted Wragg on Teachers TV via this link: www.teachers.tv/video/2615

[23] OECD (2009), *Education Today: The OECD Perspective*. Paris: OECD.

[24] David Miliband was commenting on research by Leon Feinstein, from Institute of Education, London, published in 2002, that showed the socio-economic gap was evident in children at the age of 22 months. His comments were reported in The Observer newspaper, 10 November 2002.

[25] Feinstein, Leon (2003), Inequality in Early Cognitive Development of British Children in the 1970 cohort. In *Economica* (70), 277, pp73–97.

[26] Blanden, Jo & Machin, Stephen (2008), Up and Down the Generational Income Ladder: Past Changes and Future Prospects. In *National Institute Economic Review* 205, pp101–116. A summary of their research may be found through this link: www.suttontrust.com/reports/summary.pdf

[27] Report from the Independent Commission on Social Mobility, January 2009. London: Social Mobility Commission.

[28] Hart, Betty & Risley, Todd R. (1995), *Meaningful Differences in the Everyday Experiences of Young American Children*. Baltimore, MD: Brookes Publishing. This book tells the story of a painstaking study of 42 families over a 2.5 year period. Every word spoken by the family was recorded during one full hour each month. 1,318 transcripts were coded in detail and analysed according to the family backgrounds: professional, working class or welfare (living on benefits).

[29] Fredrickson, Barbara (2009), *Positivity*. New York: Crown. This professor of psychology at the University of North Carolina suggests that positive emotions will, over time, improve learning and social interactions.

[30] Winston, Robert (2005), *A Child of Our Time*. This series of BBC documentary programmes follows the development of a group of children born in 2000. In the fifth programme, *Tried and Tested* the children start school.

[31] See the report from Independent Commission on Social Mobility (reference [26]) for a detailed analysis of research into education and social mobility, pages 36–50.

[32] Blanden, Jo; Gregg, Paul & Machin, Stephen (2005) *Intergenerational Mobility in Europe and North* America London: LSE. This research was commissioned by The Sutton Trust and completed at London School of Economics and University of Bristol.

[33] Miliband, David (2003), Class haunts classroom. In *The Guardian* 18 September 2003. The article was written when David Miliband was minister for schools. The reference for this research was not included in the article.

[34] Ginnott, Haim G. (1995), *Teacher and Child: A Book for Parents and Teachers*. New York: Collier.

[35] Mandela, Nelson (2003), *In His Own Words: From Freedom to the Future*. London: Little, Brown and Company.

Chapter Two

A threshold adventure like no other

The threshold adventurer • Maintenance or development? • Stuck schools

The threshold adventurer

Our reluctance to let ourselves go at times is illustrated vividly by Richard Bach's allegory in his book *Illusions: The Adventures of a Reluctant Messiah*.[1]

The story is about a village of creatures that live along a river bed. The water in the river flows continuously and silently all over the creatures, but they have no idea where it is going.

Every creature in the village has learned from birth to resist the flow of the water. Their way of life is preserved by clinging to things that stick at the bottom of the river.

Eventually one creature decides there must be more to life than clinging onto things. Although unable to see where the current goes, this one creature is convinced that the current knows where it is going and decides to let go and flow along with it.

The other creatures in the village ridiculed the creature and warned that the current would smash it into rocks and kill it. Safety lay in clinging on.

But the restless creature ignored them and let go. Sure enough, the creature was swept away by the current and smashed into rocks.

However, as time passed and the creature refused to cling again, the current lifted the creature free from the river bed and it was no longer hurt by crashing into rocks.

As the creature moved downstream, it came across another village with similar creatures clinging for their lives to rocks and objects on the river bed.

When they saw a creature like themselves flowing freely in the water, they thought it was a miracle and that the moving creature was a messiah come to save them.

As it passed by, the moving creature told them that it was not a messiah. The river would set them all free if they dared to let go, that life was about the voyage, the adventure. But they were too scared to let go and the creature passed by, leaving them to tell others about the legend of the moving messiah.

Teaching has been described as many things and, while, for me, the image of a weaver of magic goes nearest to describing the mystery of its power, there are other, equally potent attempts at capturing its alchemy.

For example, George Steiner refers to teaching as a craft, rather than a job. But more than that, he says it is the most privileged craft of all. Nothing else gives you the chance to stir up other people's dreams and powers, or to pass on your love for something to someone else. Only teaching gives you the opportunity to shape the future of others with what is inside you. Steiner calls it a *threshold adventure* like no other.[2]

So not just magic-weaving, nor alchemy, but threshold adventuring too.

Steve Jobs and Steve Wozniak, co-founders of Apple, embody the characteristics of threshold adventuring and have been able to survive in the highly competitive, cut-throat world of computer technology because they have never lost their ability to see opportunities and grasp them. In his speech at the MacWorld Conference and Expo in 2007, Jobs quoted ice hockey legend, Wayne Gretzky:

"I skate to where the puck is going to be, not where it has been." He went on to explain that, from the very outset, they had always tried to do precisely that at Apple. "And we always will," he promised.

Apple produced an advertisement which was a salute to the threshold adventurers whom they described as the *crazy ones*. Against a backdrop of images of such people as: Albert Einstein, John Lennon, Amelia Earhart and Andy Warhol, the voiceover pays tribute to the characters that appear.[3] The video refers to those people in history who marked themselves out by doing extraordinary things. Because they stand out, the *crazy ones* are often referred to as: misfits, rebels, trouble-makers or round pegs in square holes. Their common characteristics are that they neither defer to the status quo nor obey rules.

You may like them or hate them, quote them or disagree with them. But you cannot ignore them because it is the *crazy ones* who change things and create progress.

While some people see them as crazy, others recognise genius. It is only those people who are crazy enough to think they can change the world who actually do.

Inspired by Norman Drummond in 1997, the Columba 1400 Project was established in Staffin, on the beautiful Isle of Skye.[4] Drummond had been a BBC national governor, an army chaplain and a headteacher. To celebrate and honour the 1400th anniversary of St Columba's mission to Scotland, Drummond and his team created a community and international leadership development centre to design and deliver a range of experiences for a wide variety of people. Core to its purpose is to work with young people from tough realities and central to its principles is the belief that there is great leadership potential in those who have weathered tough times. On the Columba 1400 web-page, John Buchan sums up their aim:[5] 'Our task is not to put the greatness back into humanity, but to elicit it, for the greatness is there already.' In the leadership programme, delegates are invited to consider three powerful questions:

- Who am I?
- Why do I live and work in the way I do?
- What might I become?

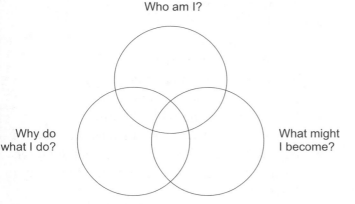

Model C: Circles of Reflection

In this reflective journey of personal development on the Isle of Skye, it is the third question which packs the punch. But it loses its potency if not preceded by the first two. The more I read about those who were called crazy, eccentric, idiosyncratic or downright foolish, the more I realise their power to go where 'the puck is going to be'.

David Hopkins describes how, in the UK over the last two decades, there has been a shift in government policy away from an age of national prescription to a culture in which schools are being asked to lead educational reform.[6] There is a developing trust in the ability of those educators actually working day-to-day, face-to-face with young people, to emerge, become creative and develop a new educational experience. One that is meaningful, relevant, fit for purpose and based squarely on a new set of values which sees academic progress as only a part and not the *raison d'être* of our education system. Perhaps the day of the threshold adventurer has come.

Threshold adventurers have many characteristics:

- strength of purpose;
- passion;
- capacity to dream;
- willingness to take risks;
- ability to live with uncertainty;
- readiness to push the boundaries;
- hopefulness without blind optimism;
- love of the questions as much as the answers;
- capacity to feel fear but not be daunted by it;
- firm commitment to a destination but ready to travel without a map;
- they dream dreams and ask why not?

A student once said to me:

"The future's important to me ... it's where I intend to spend the rest of my life."

They are often regarded as unusual, odd even, but they champion creativity and imagination.

Not a bad list of essential criteria for an appointments panel at interview.

If the context is right and ripe for new ideas, are schools, and particularly teachers, ready to take up the challenge?

Do schools and the staff who work in them have the capacity to revisit their core purpose and embark on a journey which, in a rapidly changing world, amounts simply to a continuous process of reinvention?

Do they have the courage to laugh at some of the absurdities of the system?

Is the system ready for change?

More importantly, are the people in the system up for the challenge?

Worn out by the sheer effort of survival, both personally and professionally, it is no surprise that the pan scale which has maintenance on the one side and growth, or development, on the other tips in favour of the status quo: the maintenance or development dilemma.

Maintenance or development?

Imagine ...[7]

... there is a bank that credits your account with £86,400 every morning. It carries over no balance from day-to-day. Every evening it deletes whatever part of the balance you failed to use during the day. What would you do?[8]

Each of us has such a bank. Its name is *time*.

Each day you are credited with 86,400 seconds. Every night it writes off, as lost, whatever of this you have failed to invest to good purpose. It carries over no balance. It allows no overdraft.

Each day it opens a new account for you. Each night it burns the remains of the day. If you fail to use the day's deposits, the loss is yours. There is no going back. There is no drawing against the 'tomorrow.'

You must live in the present on today's deposits. Invest it so as to get from it the utmost in health, happiness, and success. The clock is running. Make the most of today.

The value of time:

To realise the value of *one year*, ask a student who failed a grade.

To realise the value of *one month*, ask a mother who gave birth to a premature baby.

To realise the value of *one week*, ask the editor of a weekly newspaper.

To realise the value of *one hour*, ask the lovers who are waiting to meet.

To realise the value of *one minute*, ask a person who missed the train.

To realise the value of *one second*, ask a person who just avoided an accident.

To realise the value of *one-tenth of a second*, ask the person who won a silver medal at the Olympics.

Time ticks away relentlessly. My grandfather was a hero of mine. He fought in the First World War as a teenage boy and, sitting me on his knee, would tell me tales of the trenches and the Somme. He wrote poetry and drew wonderful drawings of his experiences. He told me once that he wouldn't always be with me but would always look after me. He made me promise to go outside each new year's eve, look up at the stars and click my fingers. "Why, granddad?" I asked. "Because son," he replied, "that is how fast a year goes by. Like the click of a finger. So use your time well." I am amazed each year how fast it passes and, perhaps more alarmingly, how much closer together those clicks seem to be.

My grandfather would recite Kipling's timeless piece, *If*, to me.

He was telling me to enjoy life at every opportunity and rise above the fray to see the goodness there is, even in life's darkest corners. *To fill the unforgiving minute with sixty seconds worth of distance run.*

Sadly, many people do not heed the warning and see time slip by in a blur of bustle and busyness. Paul Simon sang of 'kicking the days away'.

Too busy to dream and too frightened to dare, many individuals will go to the grave having fulfilled only a fraction of their potential; lives under-lived; dead with their song still within them. And why?

"He doesn't achieve much," a headteacher colleague once said about a member of his staff, "but he works tremendously hard at not achieving it."

In Chapter 3, I will explore what I believe is the second major reason for this failure to fulfil potential, that people simply do not believe they can, but here I want to explore the first reason: that they were just too busy.

Driven on by maintenance, doing what they've always done, so getting what they've always got, people become exhausted coping with the demands of the day. Someone once said that the only difference between a rut and a grave is the depth of the hole. If that is not depressing enough, I was reminded by a friend recently that the size of the crowd at my funeral would be determined by the weather. And I thought it would be my good deeds that would fill the place.

Maintenance has a voracious appetite, swallowing up hours, days, weeks, months and years of life, leaving many exhausted and weakened in their resolve to go in pursuit of their goals and dreams. Maintenance is also seductive. Its habitual nature sucks people into patterns of thought and action which take the shape of comfort zones. Now there is nothing wrong with habitual behaviour *per se*, habits save time. But once they fall below a level of awareness they can start to control an individual, creating default, preferred patterns of behaviour which are preferable only because that is the way they have always been done. Habits allow us to perform complex activities such as driving a car or playing a musical instrument more easily. Sports people spend hours on the practice field grooving habitual patterns of physical activity to ensure that in the heat, intensity and pressure of competition, the habit will prevail.

However, once the brain is used to a certain way of doing something and new pathways, or synaptic or electrical circuits are created, the more difficult it feels to embrace the new way. Within an individual, the deeper the grooved neural pathway, the more uncomfortable the new way seems, often leading to resistance to, and even resentment towards, what is being asked of that person. New is almost always uncomfortable. Different is not as attractive as same.

Winnie the Pooh readers may remember Edward Bear being towed downstairs by Christopher Robin, bumping his head on every step.

Edward was sure there was a better way to come down stairs, if only he could stop the bumping long enough to think about it.

Michael Fullan writes about the muddiness and messiness of change and many become stuck with their habits.[9] The latter are simply patterns of activity which, when constantly repeated, form deep neural pathways in our brain and become not only automatic but also very comfortable, like an old pair of slippers. Try folding your arms another way, or move your watch from one wrist to another. See how long it takes you to stop looking at the wrong wrist or indeed how long it takes you to put your watch back when you tire of looking at the empty space at the end of your arm.

Maintenance-driven organisations are like maintenance-driven people. They become stuck in a comfort culture, what Gerard Egan described as *the way we do things around here*.[10] As time passes, it can become increasingly difficult to unstick them. Many great ideas do not find the fertile ground in which they would thrive, not because they are flawed but simply because they are different. Given the conservative nature of schools and of those who work in them, it is hardly surprising that change of any sort is not welcomed easily.

The world of development is a different place altogether. It requires an individual to move out of the comfort zone of habit and familiarity. Eleanor Roosevelt described how every day she would try to do something out of her comfort zone because she did not want to be a stuck human being.[11] I watch people arrive at my conferences and observe them filling the room up from the back or the middle. The front row is almost always the last to be filled. Eleanor Roosevelt would have taken her seat there.

I watch delegates scanning the room to find the comfort of a friendly, known face or faces with whom to sit. Eleanor would have sought out a group in which she knew no one. Do you know what happens when a complete stranger sits amongst our group? People start shuffling around, exchanging *who on earth is this?* glances with each other.

I have a concern that in our culture people do not celebrate difference; they mistrust it. It is, I believe, at the core of racism. Different faces, strange languages, unusual clothes.

It is, I also believe, at the core of bullying. Every year about 50,000 children start at a new school in England. They wander innocently onto an asphalt playground for the first time; strapped to a bag; burdened with their parents' love; an index finger drilling away up a nostril. Someone wrote '…such pure unhappiness should be bottled and sent to all romantics.' Some of those youngsters have *bully me* written on their forehead. Why? Because they are too small, too tall, too large or too thin. They stand out. And when you stand out, others look; some stare and a few ridicule you. I grew up on the tough streets of Liverpool with red hair and glasses; I can vouch for these things.

Being different is not easy. I remember, as a teacher, daring to play music in my lessons while the students were working independently. It wasn't long before some of the older members of staff began to peer suspiciously through the glass panel of my classroom door, followed soon after by a memo from the head requiring me, as a result of several complaints from senior members of staff, to turn off the music. For maintenance read business as usual or stuckness; for development read boldness and adventure. Individuals have to get the balance right.

There will always be a need for maintenance but if the balance falls heavily towards the latter at the cost of little or no development, individuals will under-live; teams will play-it-safe; organisations will under perform and the world will be in danger of rendering its adventurers as outcasts and banishing its magic-weavers. If schools are to be or become key players in the regeneration of: our communities, our country and society as a whole, they have to become hotbeds of creativity, centres of imagination and champions of change.

The track record of schools is not encouraging. The curriculum has not seriously shifted in decades (see table below).[12] Teaching methodology has improved but much classroom practice has not changed significantly from the teaching I experienced as a boy in the sixties and seventies. Burdened with accountability processes which still place test data outcomes above all else and spread fear through classrooms and corridors of our schools, who can blame those who work there for playing it safe, teaching to the test, busying themselves in the maintenance of everyday life, holding on to the comfort zone called traditional schooling?

Comparisons of English secondary school curriculum, 1904 and 1988			
1904 regulations		**1988 national curriculum**	
English	13%	English	10%
Mathematics	13%	Mathematics	10%
Science	10%	Sciences	10-20%
Other languages	11-15%	Modern languages	10%
Housewifery	5%	Technology	10%
Manual work	5%		
History	13%	History	10%
Geography	13%	Geography	10%
Drawing	5%	Art/Music	10%
Physical education	5%	Physical education	5%

It is not, I believe, through a revolution in the systems, structures and processes of traditional schooling that real change will be achieved.

These are not unimportant, but it is in the development of the kind of people trained and appointed to work in our schools that real change will happen.

People who understand the tyranny of the present and who healthily balance maintenance with development, take risks and dare to challenge tradition.

Schools are notoriously stuck places and, cloistered and comfortable, they can be almost oblivious to the world around them. A former colleague once described to me the geography lessons he had experienced as a pupil. The teacher had the whole year's course on a role of cellophane which he stretched across an overhead projector. As the class entered lesson one in September they could hear the teacher winding the roll forward. The next day more winding - lesson two. After the final class of the year, as the class filed out for the summer holiday, they could hear the teacher rewinding the roll back to the beginning, ready for September. In a world in which 70% of the countries who sit at the United Nations did not exist 50 years ago such practice is patently absurd.[13]

But the history of schooling is not encouraging, as revealed by this series of references:[14]

Students today can't prepare bark to calculate their problems. They depend on their slates which are more expensive. What will they do when the slate is dropped and it breaks? They will be unable to write.
Teachers' Conference, 1703

Students today depend on paper too much. They don't know how to write on a slate without getting chalk dust all over themselves. They can't clean a slate properly. What will they do when they run out of paper?
Principal's Association, 1815

Students today depend too much upon ink. They don't know how to use a pen knife to sharpen a pencil. Pen and ink will never replace the pencil.
National Association of Teachers, 1907

Stuck schools

Photographer and designer Sir Cecil Beaton offers advice to resist the influence of play-it-safers. Anyone who is stuck needs to be bold, daring and different. They must release their imagination to overcome the *slaves of the ordinary* and the *creatures of commonplace*.

Students today depend upon ink from a shop. They don't know how to make their own. When they run out of ink they will be unable to write words or ciphers until their next trip to town. This is a sad commentary on modern education.

The Rural American Teacher, 1928

Students today depend on these expensive fountain pens. They can no longer write with a straight pen and nib. We parents must not allow them to wallow in such luxury to the detriment of learning how to cope in the real business world which is not so extravagant.

PTA Gazette, 1941

Ballpoint pens will be the ruin of education in our country. Students use these devices and then throw them away. The values of thrift and frugality are being discarded. Business and banks will never allow such expensive luxuries.

Federal Teachers, 1950

You can't use those calculators on the test. If I let you do that, you wouldn't ever learn how to use the tables in the back of the book and use interpolation to figure out your trig ratios.

High School Math Teacher, 1980

We can't let them use calculators in middle school. If we do, they'll forget how to do long division or how to multiply three digit numbers by three digit numbers. What will they do when they don't have access to a calculator?

Middle School Math Teacher, 1989

Why would you ever want the Internet for student use? It's just the latest fad – have them use the library.

District Employee, 1995

You don't need a web page for our school. Who's ever going to look at it? Teachers will never use email.

Teacher on a District Committee, 1996

Why do you want network drops at every teacher's desk? You're not thinking of getting a computer for all of them are you?

Building Administrator, 1999

What can you do with an LCD Projector that you can't do with an overhead projector?

Member of School Accountability Committee, 1999

Why are we talking about students having laptops in high school? I don't think most parents will even give their kids their old computer, much less buy them a new one.

School Administrator, 2000

Why would I want to put my grades on the web? Who's going to look at them?

Teacher, 2001

The 1904 regulations in England, which put together a curriculum for the future, looked, with the exception of housewifery and manual work, pretty similar to that followed by students today.

Numbers of schools, particularly in the north of England, continue to structure their holiday patterns on the old wakes weeks when the mills would close for their annual breaks. The mills are long gone but the tradition lives on.

At a conference recently, I asked the audience of teachers why we had a two-week holiday at Easter in schools. Someone shouted back, "Because they won't give us three!" The two-week Easter break grew from the agricultural tradition of lambing and planting. The farmers needed help in early spring and where better to go for cheap labour than the local school. The exercise did not take very long so after two weeks the children could return. I wonder how many children these days go lambing and planting in their Easter holidays?

Similarly, the long summer break was the result of an agricultural need to harvest the crops. A longer, more labour-intensive activity.[15]

The beginning of the school year in September grew from the traditional return of the aristocracy from their grand tour of the cultural centres of Europe during the long summer. On their return they despatched their children off to their private boarding schools and the academic year began.

The average class size of 30 came from a military belief and tradition that that was how many soldiers a sergeant could effectively control.

When Henry Ford started his car business he said that if he had asked his customers what they wanted they would have said, 'faster horses please.'[16] It is perhaps a human condition, not just the preserve of those who work in education, to be so preoccupied with what they have today (where the puck has been) rather than develop an ability to imagine the future (where the puck might be). A kind of tyranny of the present. Today is as good as it is ever going to be. The main reason for that inability, I believe, is not that people lack the imagination to think into the future, it is that they are too tired to do so.

As the result of decades of what the business writer Abrahamson called initiative overload, schools have been almost beaten into submission.[17]

Government rhetoric espouses such principles as *every child matters*, the development of the whole child and *excellence and enjoyment,* while sending into schools teams of inspectors who coldly remind headteachers that the only thing that really matters are the scores on the doors. Initiatives have rained down on schools. The government has been generous in its support of their implementation but that's not the point.

Hatch reminds us that 'human capacity, like the capacity of water, is enlarged not only by increasing the supply of training, materials and resources, but also by reducing the demand of unnecessary and excessive external initiatives.'[18] If the profession is truly to move into an age of informed professionalism, of imagination and creativity, of staff on the ground leading the reform, then something has to give. If the *crazy ones* are to emerge and the bold, the daring, the different, are to overcome the influence of the play-it-safers, the slaves of the ordinary, the creatures of the commonplace, then the shackles have to be loosened.

The signs are encouraging:
- new inspection regimes;
- the emergence of the creative curriculum;
- more understanding of how the brain works;
- new understanding about learning;
- more flexibility with the national curriculum;
- the credibility of a vocational curriculum;
- building schools for the future;
- new paradigms for how schools should function.

There is a real opportunity to begin the threshold adventure.

References and notes for Chapter 2

[1] Bach, Richard D. (1977), *Illusions: The Adventures of a Reluctant Messiah.* New York: Dell Publishing. You may read the allegory on this blog: www.coyoteprime-runningcauseicantfly.blogspot.com/2009/01/richard-bach-illusions.html

[2] Steiner, George (2003), *Lessons of the Masters.* Cambridge, MA: Harvard University Press

[3] You can see the *crazy ones* video on You Tube via this link: www.youtube.com/watch?v=Dvn_Ied9t4M

[4] Drummond, Norman (2004), *The Spirit of Success: How to connect the heart to the head in work and in life.* London: Hodder Mobius

[5] Web link to Columba 1400 is: www.columba1400.com/

[6] Hopkins, David (2007), *Every School a Great School.* Maidenhead: Open University Press. David Hopkins was chief adviser for school standards to three secretaries of state for education from 2002 to 2005.

[7] You can view this page in video via this link: www.video.aol.co.uk/video-detail/86400-seconds-in-a-day-what-will-you-do-chris-hermes/317418010

[8] Most people would say 'Draw it all out each day'

[9] Fullan, Michael (2008), *Six Secrets of Change.* San Francisco, CA: Jossey-Bass

[10] Egan, Gerard (1994), *Working the Shadow Side: A guide to positive behind-the-scenes management.* San Francisco, CA: Jossey-Bass

[11] Roosevelt, Eleanor (1958), *On My Own.* New York: Harper and Brothers

[12] The table is based on discussion in Ross, Alistair (2000) *Curriculum Construction and Critique.* London: Falmer Press. Thanks to Marcus Orlovsky and Mike Davies for their interpretations.

[13] Enriquez, Juan (2000), *As the Future Catches You: How genomics and other forces are changing your life, work, health and wealth.* New York: Crown Publishing

[14] The initial series of quotes, up to 1950, appeared in Thornburg, David (1992), *Edutrends 2010: Restructuring, Technology and the Future of Education.* Lake Barrington, IL: Starsong Publications. The later quotes were added by Karl Fisch from Arapahoe High School, Colorado. The sequence appears in his blog: www.thefischbowl.blogspot.com/2006/09/what-if.html

[15] At least one historian considers this to be an urban myth. See http://www.tes.co.uk/article.aspx?storycode=6019111

[16] Ford, Henry & Crowther, Samuel (1922), *My Life and Work.* New York: Doubleday, Page & Co. The original text has been reproduced several times, including an edition printed in 2000 North Stratford, NH: Ayer Company Publishing Inc.

[17] Abrahamson, Eric (2004), *Change Without Pain: How Managers Can Overcome Initiative Overload, Organizational Chaos and Employee Burnout.* Boston, MA: Harvard Business School Publishing

[18] Hatch, Thomas (2009), *Managing to Change: How schools can survive (and sometimes thrive) in turbulent times.* New York: Teachers College Press

Chapter Three

If the dream is big enough, the facts won't count

The card on the jar • The psychology of excellence • Dream builders or dream stealers?

The card on the jar

If it's to be, it's up to me.

The brain is an organ which starts to function the moment you are born and ceases to function the moment you stand up to speak in public.

If the inability to solve the maintenance/development dilemma leaves many unable to fulfil their potential, or the day-to-day treadmill renders them too tired to try, then the second reason why so many appear to under-live their lives is simply that they do not believe they can achieve their dreams. Choosing the safe ground, the comfort zone and the no-risk option, they dare not dream in the passionate pursuit of their goals but settle, as Frank Dick describes it, for the life of valley (not mountain) people.[1]

Part of the solution to this crisis of self-confidence and belief, both personal and collective, lies in new understanding emerging in the field of cognitive psychology. Not many people are familiar with the name of Phineas Gage, but this name features in no fewer than 60% of all books on neuro-science. The unfortunate Mr Gage suffered a terrible injury while working on a railway line in the USA in 1848.[2] Following an explosion, a pointed iron rod, 1.25 inches in diameter and 3 feet 7 inches long, weighing 7 kilos, flew towards the head of Mr Gage with great force, entering his face through the left cheek, piercing his eye socket before exiting through the top of his skull. Remarkably, Gage survived.

What fascinated doctors even more was the way in which his whole personality was transformed after the accident. The literal opening of Gage's mind offered to medical scientists new perspectives on how the brain functions. The realisation that parts of the brain could be lost or damaged, resulting in a change in personality, led to Gage's accidental injury being reproduced deliberately on countless mentally ill patients in the form of a full frontal lobotomy. A procedure made famous by the main character in the film *One Flew Over the Cuckoo's Nest*. Lobotomy was the solution to taming his rebellious nature.

Thanks to major scientific advances, particularly in the field of brain imagery and scanning, knowledge of how the brain functions has grown more in the last fifteen years than in the whole of time before that. As neuroscience continues to develop, rapid advances are being made in the fields of cognitive and self-image psychology.

Professor Albert Bandura of Stanford University, conducted much research into the concept of self-efficacy, the belief in the ability of individuals to make things happen in their lives.[3] Highly efficacious individuals believe that the locus of control lies within and is not external to them. They cause things to happen proactively, not waiting for other people, circumstances, fate or luck to deal out life's cards to them. In short, they are actors not reactors.

Key to the notion of self-efficacy is the power of the beliefs an individual holds. Such beliefs can be held individually or collectively. They can help people and organisations grow and develop or can hamper and hold them back.

Fleas can jump huge heights in proportion to their body size. But, curiously, if they are placed into a jar with a card placed over it, after repeatedly hitting the card, when the latter is removed, the fleas jump no higher than the height of the card even though it is no longer there.

A bear, transported in a cage to a zoo in the US, was lowered into the bear pit. Its keepers decided to leave the cage bars there for 24 hours enabling it to become familiar with its new surroundings. When the bars were removed the bear would not move from the platform even though it was no longer penned in.

Elephants in India are trained by being tethered with a rope to a stake in the ground. As the elephant attempts to move away, the tug of the rope sends it back to the stake. Amazingly, when the rope is eventually removed the elephant walks as far as the rope allowed and no further, even though it is no longer restrained.

We should never underestimate the power of beliefs; they do not have to be true, we just have to believe that they are to determine our behaviour, aspiration and achievement. There is no such thing as the truth in the world of belief, just the truth as we perceive it to be. How many imagined barriers have held back so many individuals from the pursuit of their dreams?

> Don't die with the
> music in you.
>
> Wayne Bennett

- What bars currently hold you trapped?
- What ropes tether you?
- What cards sit menacingly on your jar?

They do not have to be real to restrain you; you just have to believe they are. The power of beliefs should never be underestimated.

There are many famous examples of people who refused to be held back by limiting beliefs and who refused to die with the music in them. History is littered with such stories and here are some of my favourites:

Henry Ford experienced two major business failures before the creation and mass production success of his Model T.

Arthur Davidson and William Harley were told to stay out of the garage for good (which they had been using to build a motorcycle) when one of their carburettors exploded. And when they finally did finish making their first bike, they had doors slammed in their faces when trying to raise money, door to door, for mass production.

Beethoven was once declared hopeless at 'composing' by his music teacher.

Walt Disney originally created a character named Oswald the Rabbit. When he went to his distributor to negotiate a better rate for the creation of the character, he found out that he didn't own the rights to the character and that the distributor did. Furthermore, that same distributor stole employees right out from under him by offering them better pay. And after this major setback, Disney went on to create Mickey Mouse.

Steve Jobs was fired from the company he helped create, Apple, because executives saw him as too inexperienced and eccentric to entrust him with a current major undertaking (the Lisa project), and he had no formal business education. Jobs then founded the company NeXT, which was later purchased by Apple for $402 million dollars. In 2000, he was named permanent CEO of Apple, responsible for the iPod, iTunes and the new iPhone.

Charlotte Brontë was reviewed in 1849 thus; "In Wuthering Heights, all the faults of Jane Eyre are magnified a thousand-fold, and the only consolation is that it will never be read."

Einstein's parents worried that he was sub-normal.

Elvis Presley was fired by The Grand Old Opry after only one performance. He was told, "You ain't going nowhere, son. You ought to go back to driving a truck."

Michael Jordan was kicked off his high school basketball team.

Stephen King threw his manuscript, Carrie, in the garbage because he was tired of the rejections. In fact he gave up posting his rejection slips on the bulletin board above his computer once they were too thick for a pin.

Oprah Winfrey was rejected for the first news anchor position she applied for because she was African-American and overweight.

John Grisham, best-selling author, was rejected by 16 agents and a dozen publishing houses before his novel, *A Time to Kill*, was accepted.

Marilyn Monroe was turned down by a modelling agency and was told that she'd better learn to do secretarial work or get married because she didn't have a future in show business.

How much more impoverished would the world have been had this gallery of famous people listened to the dream-stealers; believed their script; bought their version of the truth; lacked the courage and resilience to dream their dreams and say 'why not?' We may not all be Walt Disney or Charlotte Brontë but we are all capable of choosing to be the best we can be by believing in ourselves.

Both the developing knowledge of how the brain functions and the deeper understanding of the power of self-efficacy, underpinned by self-belief, have given a clearer insight in to the secrets of high performance. Why do some people reach for the stars while so many settle for the moon?

In her book *Be Your Own Life Coach* Fiona Harold confirms the power of self-belief by reminding us that we all know people who achieve remarkable things, not because they have more talent but because they have more desire and belief.[4]

There are important messages for educators here. The development of self-belief, causality and confidence in young people is central to their success. But in a system which still produces winners and losers (the proportion of young people who achieve five GCSEs grades A*–C in England continues to hover between 50% and 60%) tough questions have to be asked about our core purpose.

If we are preparing students for life and not just exams, then where in the curriculum experience of our young is there space to develop an awareness of what their beliefs are? And to nurture an understanding of the influence such beliefs, such 'truths' hold over them and their chances of success? Self-efficacy has a clear case for its introduction as a compulsory area of study in any curriculum.

Unfortunately, as Andy Hargreaves reminds us, such skills, pushed aside by the relentless pursuit of curriculum content, happen by accident in schools not on purpose.[5] They are random, not strategic.

The psychology of excellence

The development of neuro-linguistic programming (NLP) has deepened even further our grasp of high performance. This concept emerged in the early seventies with the work of Richard Bandler and John Grinder at the University of California, in Santa Cruz.[6] It is known as the psychology of excellence.

NLP has a number of important presuppositions, including the power of self-efficacy and self-belief. Perhaps the most significant is the claim that we create from our life experience our own unique model of the world, our map of reality.

Most people spend their lives following the route mapped out by their beliefs, manifest in their values and attitudes, behaving not in accordance with some sort of eternal truth but simply the truth as they perceive it to be – however stifling and limiting that may be. The challenge is clear: if we can modify such beliefs by changing our reality map, would it be possible to improve self-efficacy and give ourselves not only more choices but also improve dramatically the way we perform?[7]

Part of the solution to this question lies in an understanding of how human beings experience the world. Tice and Steinberg describe this process (see Model D, p64).[8]

Through our conscious mind via the senses of: smell, touch, feel, sight and hearing, we filter the evidence before us;
- *Perception* – what am I experiencing here?

The sum total of such experience is stored in our subconscious. The interplay of the conscious and subconscious takes an individual on an intriguing journey towards the formulation of attitudes, values and beliefs. For not only are experiences stored but, more crucially, so are the emotions associated with such experience;

- *Association* – where have I experienced this before and how did I feel at that moment?

Although knowledge of how memory functions is still scant, psychologists believe that we do not forget anything, that memories lie as a huge database deep within the hard drive of our mind. Though many are forgotten in the conscious mind, skilful hypnotists can enable individuals to regress and recall deep, powerful, hitherto-hidden experiences and emotions. These have not only shaped the way individuals are but, more importantly, what they believe about themselves and the world around them.

Within seconds a piece of long forgotten music can reduce to tears people who, until that moment, were perfectly content, as it drags from our emotional memory store (the amygdala) recollections of: that person, that relationship, that moment in time. It is because of this powerful process of association that we tend not to live our lives according to how we could be, but how we have been. An understanding of this dynamic is crucial not only to those who work with young people but also to all those involved in the leadership of change.

If perception and association are about real experiences plucked from the huge database of our personal history, then the consequent judgement and assessment we make of them;

- *Evaluation* – did this experience feel good or bad?

determine the way we decide;

- *Decision* – what should I believe as a result of how I feel?

and finally, what I do as a result
- *Action* – how should I now behave?

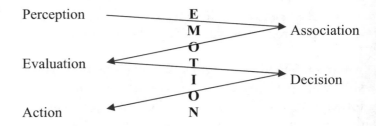

Model D: How humans experience the world

Such a process maps out the route by which we arrive at our attitudes, values and beliefs; our truth, our unique view of how the world is and, more crucially, how it should be. Put simply, our belief system.

Interestingly, a prime characteristic of the subconscious is that it cannot distinguish between what is real and what is imaginary; what is true and what is false, so whether the powerful beliefs we hold are true or not becomes irrelevant.

The term subconscious, not to be confused with unconscious, is used widely and has no precise definition. Consequently, it is avoided in scientific or academic writing. It commonly refers to a level of perception that in some sense is beneath our conscious awareness.

We all recognise our conscious mind when we are thinking or how we are feeling at any moment. But sometimes we may not be aware of what stimulated the thought or emotion. And the same stimulus may trigger different thoughts and emotions in different people. It is believed that our individual thoughts and emotions are triggered by our subconscious mind.

Our subconscious mind is the sum total of our experience to date. It is unique because everyone has a different set of experiences through life. We are prone to react in certain ways when faced with a particular situation depending on the tendencies in our subconscious mind and this shapes our character. It also means that while we cannot alter our subconscious today, we can develop it in future by purposefully choosing our next experiences.

I am reminded of a gardening analogy. When we pot new plants, or sow new seeds, we are unaware of the other seeds present in the compost or soil. As we water our seeds and provide them with sunlight, we soon find weeds popping up, stimulated by the external conditions. The weeds are like the thoughts and feelings that pop out of our subconscious.

I often cry during sad movies and always feel a real sense of fear when the Zulu army finally appears on the ridge overlooking Rawke's Drift. I have friends who unashamedly jump on chairs when a mouse scurries across the floor, even though the conscious mind knows we are only watching a movie or that the mouse cannot harm us. The powerful subconscious mind exerts an influence over the conscious mind and causes us to behave as if the experience is vivid, present and real.

No such thing as the truth, remember, just the truth as we believe it to be. A key question is whether it is possible to change such perceptions; to improve the way we see ourselves; to adapt and change our beliefs about ourselves and the world as we see it?

If not, then all theories of self-efficacy can be thrown overboard, and, the lucky few apart, we would be condemned to drift helplessly, unable to shape our future, draw our own map or redesign our future.

Of course psychologists, therapists, coaches and teachers know that this is not the case and a huge multi-million dollar business has grown up around the self-help industry. The message is clear. It is possible to affect and change the way we are, what we believe and how we behave. There are patterns of behaviour which are hard-wired forming part of our first nature, our hard-drive, our inherited characteristics and our genetic make-up. But that is only part of the picture. For we have a second nature which can be changed and shaped to become a powerful influence over our first nature.

Barbara Fredrickson in her research on happiness claims that our genetic make-up and natural disposition account for about 50% of the way we are.[9] A further 10 % is determined by the context in which we find ourselves but a significant 40% is intentional. That means we can change, modify and develop it. Second nature is often described as what we choose to do with our pre-determined, first nature.

There are people who deny this power to change and develop, abdicating responsibility with phrases such as: 'I'm sorry, I can't help it, it's just the way I am', or, 'You know what I'm like.' These responses contradict concepts such as self-efficacy. We can shape our own destiny and become the person we wish to be. But how?

Leon Festinger, a leading research psychologist, did much work around the area of cognitive dissonance, the theory that the conscious mind of an individual cannot hold two opposing ideas or conflicting beliefs at the same time.[10] Such conflict or dissonance creates neuro-physical as well as psychological tension when our system is thrown 'out of order' (discrepancy production).

There is a dimension of the subconscious known as the creative subconscious. Among its key functions is to maintain order in our lives. When our system is thrown out of order by an alternative vision of how things could or should be, energy and power is created within the individual to resolve the tension and put things back in order, the way they should be (discrepancy reduction) or move to the new, preferred state. Gestalt psychologists often call this the 'out-of-order-into-order-process.'[11]

Observe how, when we see paintings on the wall which are not quite straight, we move to straighten them, to restore the order of things. Conversely, if there is no discrepancy, no problem and no disorder then there will be no desire, no energy produced, to restore the old or create the new. It is simply not needed. The expression *comfort zone* is used to describe this state.

That individuals prefer to stay in their comfort zone is understandable. But it is not difficult to see the potential of such a process were it to be used deliberately to cause such creative tension. Efficacious people, either individually or in groups, often deliberately create such dissonance, move to the edge of their comfort zone and strategically produce discrepancy. They begin by graphically describing a new order of things, a better way to be, a powerful alternative to current reality.

Through words (affirmation) or pictures (visualisation), the most skilful behave as if they have already achieved the desired state by describing what, in the present tense, they are thinking, feeling, saying and doing when they have succeeded. If sufficiently skilful, they can harness the creative energies and frustrations required to unstick people, create discrepancy and unleash their teleological nature. They can help and encourage individuals, teams and whole organisations to move towards a new order, a new picture and a new vision. Indeed, I would argue that this is a key first step in the change dynamic.

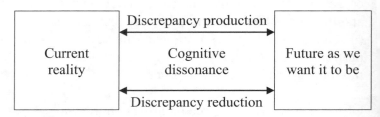

Model E: Change dynamics

Most books on leadership or the management of change reinforce the crucial need to set goals and objectives. They are right. What most of them fail to do is take the reader through why the goal-setting, dream-building cycle is a necessary first step, based on sound psychological understanding, rooted in human neural behaviour and crucial to any enduring change.

It is tempting in our hectic lives both professionally and personally, to rush through or even skip this stage: a serious flaw if the goal is permanent, lasting change that starts out in the second nature but with practice and application can become part of our first nature, our hard-wiring, our habit and our natural behaviour. This is core to the production of high performance and essential understanding for anyone involved in the teaching or coaching business.

Developing the ability to dream dreams and say 'why not?' is vital to any human endeavour. Admiral Jim Stockdale was imprisoned for eight years during the war in Vietnam.[12] Tortured regularly, along with his fellow inmates, he created a system to enable the men to survive the experience by using goals.

He explained that no one could survive torture indefinitely, so he devised a process whereby they could reveal a little information after a pre-determined time. This gave the men small goals to survive toward.

When he was asked who first succumbed to the pain and degradation, he replied, "That's easy – it was the optimists." He never, as they did, confused "faith that you will prevail in the end" with blind optimism. Unlike the optimists, he was able to confront the harsh reality of day-to-day life in captivity while always preserving a hope that one day he would be free and back with his family.

The message is simple and profound; however difficult your current reality, if you can be completely honest about it, it is your ability to stay goal-oriented and hopeful that will help you to prevail. Jim Collins described his meeting with Admiral Stockdale as having a profound influence on his own development.[13]

Collins acknowledges that everyone experiences setbacks, disappointments and devastating events in life that are unexpected, without reason and beyond blame. They may involve a serious accident or contracting a harmful disease, possibly losing a loved one. It could be losing a job through a political upheaval or, as in Stockdale's case, being captured in Vietnam and imprisoned for eight years.

Dream builders or dream stealers?

Jules Verne, the famous science fiction author, once remarked that while some people dream and ask 'why?' when he dreamt of things he asked 'why not?'

69

What Collins learned from Stockdale was it's not the degree of difficulty that people face which distinguishes them but rather it is the way they deal with it.

The ability to retain your faith that you will eventually overcome the hardship, while simultaneously dealing with the vicious reality of it, has proved time and again that you will recover from the hardship as a stronger, not weaker, person. Collins refers to this ability as the *Stockdale Paradox*.

Recently, a colleague commented wryly that if she had used the word 'vision' ten years ago she would have been locked away, and now she can't get a job without one.

Words such as 'dreams', 'vision' and 'mission' have never really been popular in schools. Staffs' eyes glaze over when they hear them or more cynically tick another box on the card of that favourite game amongst the staffroom cynics, buzzword bingo.[14] As a result they are often replaced by 'goals', 'objectives' or 'outcomes'. My view is that there is a power and a poetry in words such as 'dreams' that touches people emotionally in a way that their replacements cannot.

After all, Martin Luther King did not stand at the Lincoln Memorial before 200,000 people and say, "I have a strategic plan."

I used to be called upon to help schools that were in difficulty to find their way out of the sometimes serious predicament in which they found themselves. One first suggestion I would make would be to buy a bottle of quality champagne, place it in the staffroom fridge and ask each member of staff to touch the bottle each day to feel how much colder it was. The colder it became, the stronger the desire to open it, the greater the need to improve and justify the reward of finally opening it. Staff reported how each touch increased the dissonance while strengthening their resolve to one day achieve their goal. The more powerful the image, the more potent the emotion and the greater the desire to achieve.

Michael Fullan describes the power of hope in the context of education:[15]

> *Principals with hope are much less likely to succumb to the daily stresses of the job. They place their problems in a loftier perspective that enables them to rebound from bad days. Once leaders realise that having hope is not a prediction, that it is independent of knowing how things might turn out, it becomes a deeper resource. Leaders with hope are less likely to panic when faced with immediate and pressing problems. It is especially important that leaders have and display hope, that they show that they are prepared to fight for lost causes, because they set the tone for so many others. Teachers are desperate for lifelines of hope...*
>
> *... Articulating and discussing hope when the going gets rough re-energises teachers, reduces stress and can point to new directions. Principals will be much more effective (and healthier) if they develop and pursue high hopes...*

Take an elastic band, put your palms together and wrap it around your hands. Keeping one hand still move the other upwards to feel the band tense and stretch. Imagine that the static hand is current reality, where you are now. The tension is the energy created by a move to another goal, the future as you want it to be. As the band stretches, the tension has to be released to prevent the elastic from snapping. Either the static hand must move upwards or the moving hand must move back towards the other. Which does which, will depend upon the more powerful of the two.

If current reality is too attractive and the desire to stay put too strong, then status quo will prevail and where you are is where you stay. On the other hand, as the image of the preferred future grows stronger, irresistible even, then status quo can no longer be an option and you will not be able to live with the frustration of current reality. To move or to stay is a simple choice but the power of 'beginning with the end in mind' (Stephen Covey[16]) should never be under-estimated. It is tempting to short-circuit what sports people call end-game thinking.

There are plenty who will resist the process with such phrases as: 'Now let's be realistic'; 'I'm not being negative but…' or 'How much is all of this going to cost?' But time spent focusing on the outcome, clarifying the vision, enhancing the tension and embedding the desire to succeed, if handled successfully, will pay rich dividends in the change game. The clearer the vision, the more vivid the gap between where we are and where we want to be, the more power and energy will be released in the creative subconscious to resolve the tension.

However, a word of caution from Michael Fullan.[17] The clarity of vision that we seek to share is more an outcome of the change process than a prerequisite. In other words, let the cognitive dissonance work for itself and don't spend too much time trying to develop a shared vision to begin with.

The world of marketing has long since harnessed such understandings to make us feel we are sitting in that car, going on that holiday or living in that house. The power can be such that some people find themselves in difficult financial situations by borrowing too much to obtain their dream.

It is a grasp of the power of such processes that will enable leaders to believe they can bring about change even in seemingly intransigent people: how parents can make an impact on even the most stubborn of children; how teachers can seriously affect the lives of their students by skilfully harnessing dreams and aspirations. Magic-weaving is not accidental; it is rooted in positive psychology.

The burning question then is: *Is it possible to create within our subconscious alternative images, dreams or goals to compete with what can be for many the negative reality of day-to-day existence?*

I want to present this notion another way. The psychological tension felt, when individuals bring about this state of mind deliberately, is key to the adoption of new beliefs, the charting of a new map and the creation of another reality.

Over the last 25 years, psychologists have researched these dimensions of the mind seeking to understand and harness its power. As a result, in the world of sport, great coaches have taught athletes to harness such techniques as visualisation and goal-setting to enhance performance and move to new peaks and levels. They strive to develop their self-efficacy; work tirelessly on their teleological nature by moving from the current reality of their performance, through discrepancy production and the graphic agreement of desired goals. They stand by and support their protégés as the energy and power created by the gap between where they are and where the wish to be drives them to newer heights (discrepancy reduction). They celebrate milestones on the journey of achievement before setting new goals and agreeing new frontiers.

Sounds very much like assessment for learning to me; where your own PB (personal best) is paramount and you measure yourself against yourself. Most athletes do not go to the Olympic Games to win a medal. After all, a very small minority actually do. They go to produce a time, distance, height, weight or level that they have never achieved before. I believe strongly that if such processes work so effectively in the arenas of sport then they can work in the learning spaces and examination rooms of our schools. Performance can be enhanced in any context if the coach/teacher/mentor/parent makes skilful use of such processes.

Worryingly, the reverse is also true. Great damage can be visited on individuals through the sustained use of labelling, criticism, denigration, put-downs or what some students call 'killer statements'.

The message is clear. We can improve our self-efficacy:

- by understanding why we believe what we believe;
- by having the courage and support to change the belief; by creating new 'truths';
- by redrawing new maps of our reality and of our place in the world.

In other words we can reinvent our future, stop under-performing and under-living our lives. It's a simple choice. We have the power to take control of our lives and create our own future. It is not easy but it is doable. The good news is the skills required to do this are teachable and learnable. The bad news is it is very difficult to do this on your own.

What is required is a new dialogue about the moral purpose of our schools with a clear focus on the role of the adults in them. In the hands of the right people, students may be empowered to change their perception of themselves and improve their internal image. In the company and care of magic-weavers, their potential can be released in ways we never imagined. The bold and possibly over-ambitious aim in the school's mission statement, that each individual will fulfil his or her potential, may be more within reach.

But such magicians and wizards must be rare indeed? Not so. Our corridors, playgrounds, classrooms and school halls already team with them. They have always been there. But only now, as the result of our new understanding about the brain and its functions, does it appear that high performance is neither accidental nor the exclusive domain of the gifted and talented. It is available to all those who, under the coaching of the right people, dare to believe they can.

So, how does the magic function?

How does the alchemy work?

References and notes for Chapter 3

[1] Dick, Frank (2006), *Winning: Motivation for Business, Sport and Life*. Richmond, Surrey: Abingdon Management & Consulting. Dr Frank Dick is president of the European Athletics Coaches Association and was formerly coach to Boris Becker and Daley Thompson. He is renowned for his motivational skills.

[2] Macmillan, Malcolm (2000), *An Odd Kind of Fame: Stories of Phineas Gage*. Cambridge, MA: MIT Press. A website about Phineas Gage has been created by the same author, see: www.deakin.edu.au/hmnbs/psychology/gagepage/

[3] Bandura, Albert (1994), Self-efficacy. In Ramachaudran, V.S. (Ed), *Encyclopaedia of Human Behaviour* Vol.4 pp71–81. A copy of the original article is available on the web, see: www.des.emory.edu/mfp/BanEncy.html

[4] Harold, Fiona (2001), *Be Your Own Life Coach: How to Take Control of Your Life and Achieve Your Wildest Dreams*. London: Hodder & Stoughton

[5] Hargreaves, Andy and Shirley, Dennis (2009), *The Fourth Way: The Inspiring Future for Educational Change*. Thousand Oaks, CA: Corwin Press

[6] Bandler, Richard and Grinder, John (1983), *Reframing: Neuro-Linguistic Programming and the Transformation of Meaning*. Moab, UT: Real People Press . See also this website about NLP: www.nlpacademy.co.uk/WhatisNLP.asp

[7] As with many other ideas about our minds and how they work, NLP attracts sceptics. In the interest of presenting a balanced view about this theory, here is a link to one of the sceptics to help you form your own opinion: www.skepdic.com/neurolin.html

[8] Tice, Louis E. and Steinberg, Alan (1989), *A Better World, a Better You: The Proven Lou Tice "Investment in Excellence" Program*. New Jersey: Prentice Hall Professional Technical Reference

[9] Fredrickson, Barbara (2009), *Positivity: Groundbreaking Research Reveals How to Embrace the Hidden Strength of Positive Emotions, Overcome Negativity and Thrive*. New York: Crown Publishing

[10] Festinger, Leon (1957), *A theory of cognitive dissonance*. Stanford, CA: Stanford University Press. This is the seminal text about cognitive dissonance. There are many websites that provide more readily available information. For example: www.changingminds.org/explanations/theories/cognitive_dissonance.htm

[11] As with NLP, see [7] above, cognitive dissonance also attracts some sceptics. Once again, here is a link to help you form your own views about the topic: www.skepdic.com/cognitivedissonance.html

[12] Stockdale, James B. (1993), *Courage Under Fire: Testing Epictetus's Doctrines in a Laboratory of Human Behaviour.* Stanford, CA: Hoover Institution on War, Revolution and Peace. The official website for James Stockdale is: www.admiralstockdale.com/

[13] Collins, Jim (2001), *Good to Great.* New York: HarperCollins

[14] You can find a buzzword bingo card suitable for most situations from this website: www.bullshitbingo.net/cards/

[15] Fullan, Michael (1998), Leadership for the 21st Century. In *Education Leadership* vol.55, no.7

[16] Covey, Stephen R. (1989), *7 Habits of Highly Effective People.* London: Simon & Shuster

[17] Fullan, Michael (2010), *Motion Leadership.* Thousand Oaks, CA: Corwin

Chapter Four

The voice in your head

Whether you think you can or you can't, you're right • The parent trap • The teacher trap

Whether you think you can or you can't, you're right

"I am part of all that I have met;
Yet all experience is an arch wherethro'
Gleams that untravell'd world, whose margin fades
For ever and for ever when I move."

From *Ulysses* by Alfred Lord Tennyson

If our developing knowledge of high performance is to be useful, it has to become accessible and digestible to those outside the complex and sometimes mysterious world of cognitive psychology theory. I use a simple map (Model F) to pull together the concepts outlined in Chapter 3, and help chart a way through what can be a bewildering process.

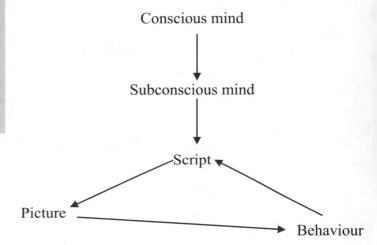

Model F: The dimensions of your mind

From the womb, our experience of the world filters, via the senses, through our conscious mind into the subconscious. From moment to moment, as the conscious and subconscious interact, a continuous drama is played out through a process of perception, association, evaluation, decision and action.

As a result, we form from experience: our attitudes, values and beliefs. These are often described as: our version of reality; our unique map of the world; our truth; our self-talk; or our script.[1] They enable us to make sense of the world and, more importantly, to understand our place within it.

The script in this drama is central to how we interpret the world and make judgements about people, actions and events. Benjamin Zander describes the script as the *voice in your head*.[2] If you are wondering now what he means by the voice in your head, then that, he points out, is the voice in your head. Each voice plays to a unique script, he claims, from the moment you are born until the moment you die. The only advantage to dying, Zander states wryly, is that it stops – we think. It plays on a continuous loop: 50,000 thoughts a day, 24 hours a day, seven days a week, 365 days a year.

If magic-weaving is to become the norm and not the exception, then it is crucial for all those who work in the development of young people to have, at least:

- a rudimentary knowledge of how the mind works;
- an understanding of why some succeed while others fail; and, most importantly,
- the ability to grasp the power this script, this voice in our head, exerts over the way we behave and what we achieve.

The script is the catalyst in a process often referred to as the *self-talk cycle*; self-talk creating a self-image which produces a performance that results in more self-talk.[3] I prefer the script-picture-behaviour-script cycle (Model F).

We are the sum total of our experience. Our script, or the voice in our head, determines not only how we see ourselves, but also what we believe about ourselves and, consequently, how we behave. It is clear that if the self-talk is negative and the self-image low then our behaviour, our performance, will deteriorate. If in our lives we have suffered more discouragement than encouragement and accepted the destructive views of others, then negative scripts can become grooved in our subconscious.[4] What is clear is that if we do not have the ability to take control of our script, that script will control us. For many the self-talk is toxic. When faced with a challenge such people are beaten before they start. Lou Tice says that if other people talked to us the way we sometimes talk to ourselves they would be up for abuse and defamation of character.[5]

I once mentored a student for his GCSE examinations and his first response was:

"No use mentoring me, all my results will be like submarines."

"Submarines?" I replied, somewhat confused.

"Yeah," came the riposte, "all below sea-level."

Those familiar with the English GCSE examinations will realise immediately that level C is the recognised pass mark he had to achieve. Though I laughed, I was aware of the toxic power of such self-deprecating words and we spent a good deal of time rewriting his script.

Just as the maintenance/development dilemma can leave people too tired to dream, so the lack of awareness about the power of the script-picture-behaviour-script cycle can render individuals powerless to improve and develop. There is nothing wrong with habitual maintenance, it saves time, and we all have and need a script. But if the two fall below our level of awareness, remaining hidden within the subconscious, they will exercise a powerful control over us, leaving us unable or indeed unwilling to change our lives.

For decades sports coaches have understood the power of this script-picture-behaviour-script cycle. During an international training session, one such coach called over a young swimmer for a word.

"Listen carefully," he whispered, "I have something extremely important I need to tell you and you need to understand. When you get to the Olympic final there will come a moment during that race when you will be three metres from your dream.[6] Show me three metres," he said, and they paced them out together.

"Turn around," he continued. "Now put out your arm." The youngster obeyed, still bemused.

"See, one metre has gone already. Now you are only two metres away from the finish wall, from that dream. I must warn you now that at that stage in the race you will be completely alone." The young swimmer looked concerned.

"Oh, don't worry," he continued, "I will be there poolside with your family and friends screaming encouragement. Millions of viewers all over the world will be shouting at plasma screens but you won't hear a thing. You will be…" "In the zone," the young swimmer whispered, finishing the sentence for him.

"Exactly. And you need to know, too, that you will be drained physically. You will have given me everything." The swimmer nodded fervently.

"Every nerve, muscle, tendon and sinew will be crying out for you to stop," he continued. "There is only one thing that will carry you that final, two, silent, lonely metres to your dream. What is it?" he asked.

"The voice in my head," came the intense response.

"Exactly," he went on. "We've four years to write that script. Just enough time. Let's start right now."

Carl Lewis, the sprinter and long jumper who won nine Olympic gold medals, refused to believe scientists' claims that it was impossible to jump 30 feet because thoughts like that had a way of sinking into his feet.

Before Roger Bannister broke the four-minute mile barrier in May 1954 there was a generally held belief in scientific as well as athletic circles that the feat was simply not possible and might even pose a threat to the life of anyone who attempted it. The script was clear – it just could not be done. But Bannister had his own goals and dreams; he wrote his own script. Highly driven, his self-belief and self-talk enabled him to see the success even before he had achieved it and were core to his superhuman performance.

He went on to run the mile in three minutes 59.4 seconds. Bannister was the embodiment of the threshold adventurer. Curiously, it took little time for the magic he weaved to rub off on others.

Although no one in the history of athletics had ever achieved such a feat before, within seven months of that historic event, no fewer than 37 other runners went on to break the four-minute barrier, achieving the unachievable, believing the unbelievable. Bannister had taken the card off the jar and changed the script forever.

Although having the right script is key to performance, having the right scriptwriters around you is equally important. What is surprising is that most will live out their lives according to a script which was probably written by someone else. So who are these script writers? Well, they are all around you.

For many, parents were the first scriptwriters. My mother is an old Liverpool warrior, now in her eighties. I have nothing but the deepest love for my mum who, after the death of my father when I was ten, brought up my brother Tom and me almost single-handedly in one of the toughest areas of Liverpool. But when I am with her I sometimes feel 12 years old. My stepfather, Bill, joked recently, "Don't worry about it John, when I'm with her I'm ten."

I went to see her recently and before I could say 'hello' she had told me to get my hair cut and wondered why I was wearing that suit - the colour was wrong for me. From time to time she says, "John, you know how you are," and reminds me that she is only telling me "for my own good."

I have learned to surf her comments and poke harmless fun in her direction from time to time but, more important, I have learned to process them against my own script. For many, though, parents still hold too powerful a sway over them. I am not saying that parental advice should be either shunned or avoided. But it should be received and tempered by young people who have been raised by the same parents to consider the opinions of others while preserving both their self-efficacy and their right to make up their own mind.

The parent trap

Having one child makes you a parent ...

... having two makes you a referee.

Parents carry photos for everyone to see, in compartments in their wallets where the money used to be.

Teachers need to heed the same advice. One of my former teachers would scoff at this notion. He would remind us of the old adage he had pinned to his classroom wall:

Rule One: The referee is always right.
Rule Two: When the referee is wrong, rule one applies.

"For 'referee' read 'teacher'," he would sneer, prodding the word with an admonishing, right index finger.

Successful parenting, like teaching, is like leading. It is the ability:

- to be the head of questions and not answers;
- to offer advice only when it is sought;
- to let people make and learn from mistakes;
- to stay close to them when they fail;
- to refuse to let advice, welcome or not, stifle creativity;
- to understand the empowering nature of the answer 'I have no idea';
- to let them experience the joy of doing it for themselves;
- to enable them to feel the exhilaration of freedom and independence, of knowing that they no longer need you.

Paradoxically, I believe that from that very moment they will start to need you more than ever.

As a parent, I know how difficult it is to resist writing a script for your children. It was only recently when I saw a poster in a school foyer that I solved a personal dilemma with one of my own sons. He appeared to be squandering his talent and was in danger of dropping out. The more advice I felt the need to give, the greater the gap between us. Cat Stevens' famous song *Father and Son* kept playing in my head.

The poster showed two young children seated with a parent standing behind them. The caption was simple and, for me, personally, profound in its impact. It read:

'Help me to become the person I can be and not the person you want me to be.'

From that moment I stopped giving advice and trying to change him. At first, he couldn't understand the difference in my attitude and kept asking me, "Dad, are you alright?" But, hard as it was for me, I persevered. Then, strangely, for the first time in a long time he began to talk through his ideas, seek my advice and share his hopes and worries. He hadn't noticed but I had stopped trying to write his script for him and was trying to help him create his own.

---

7 things children learn from their parents

1. That money does not grow on trees
2. That I wasn't born in a barn
3. That I'm not deaf
4. That if the wind changed my expression would stick
5. That I could smile on the other side of my face
6. That if I didn't stop crying I would be given something to cry about
7. That they weren't born yesterday

The teacher trap

Teachers, too, are powerful, influential script-writers. Individuals consistently approach me at or after conferences to share their script-writing stories, both positive and negative.

On a visit to a school, I met the art coordinator and chatted about her career as an art teacher. She had gained a good honours degree in art from university but enjoyed telling me that she had become interested in the subject by mistake. Apparently, when she was seven-years-old the headteacher had written to her mother to request a meeting to discuss her daughter's progress. Accompanying her to the meeting, she sat in silence as the head explained to her mother that they thought her daughter might be autistic. "I heard 'artistic'," she laughed. In contrast to her mother, she floated out of the room buoyed by the head's belief in her. The fears of autism were unfounded but the belief in her ability as an artist remained.

De-coding teacher-speak
(What teachers really mean on parents' evening)

Satisfactory progress...	*I can't think of a single interesting thing to say about him*
Expresses herself confidently...	*Cheeky little madam*
Easily influenced...	*The class fall-guy*
A vivid imagination...	*Never short of an excuse*
Reliable...	*Grasses on his mates*
Works better in a small group...	*Can't take my eyes off him for a minute*
Inclined to daydream...	*In one ear and out the other*
A born leader...	*Runs a protection racket*

My colleague Alistair Smith told me the story of a large ten-form entry high school in England.[7] The mathematics department prided itself on its ability to set (track) the students accurately by their ability. When the GCSE examination results arrived each year they produced a table of results within the department to check the system. Sure enough, students from Set 1 were at the top and those in Set 10 were at the bottom. There they were, in accurate chronological order, except that the students in Set 4 finished higher than those in Set2. For one group to jump two levels was unprecedented.

So the inquest began into what amazing things the Set 4 teacher had done to achieve the feat.

"Oh don't thank me," she said, "I thought I was teaching Set 2." She had made a mistake. Having placed the card higher on the jar, she had helped the fleas jump to the new height.

Her only regret, she claimed, was that she hadn't thought she was teaching Set 1.

It is easy to see how negative scripts and pictures can be destructive and cause performance to spiral downwards. The young are particularly vulnerable to the opinions of others. As they grow up, friends, relations, teachers, parents and peers offer advice and express views on how good or bad, clever or stupid, talented or useless they are. As a result, while not overtly agreeing with such views, young people will frequently be affected by them and, in psychological terms, give sanction to them. Such evaluations can humiliate or humour, hurt or heal; but whether negative or positive their power should never be underestimated.

Eleanor Roosevelt claimed that no one can upset you unless you give them permission to do so.[8] Unfortunately such resilience is often absent in young people during the vulnerable years of childhood and adolescence. Understanding of the power of such interactions is essential knowledge for parents and should be compulsory in the training of coaches and teachers.

When my friend Sue, a retired headteacher, was six-years-old she was asked to line up in a primary school classroom by her teacher who announced that she was going to ask the group to sing. Excitedly, Sue, who loved singing, joined the line.

"While you are singing I am going to come down the line to listen to each of you," the teacher explained, "and if I put my hand on your head, you are to stop singing and mouth the words."

The message was stark and brutal. Sue, standing in the middle of the line, described how the teacher stood before her and then stooped to listen. Sue recalls the moment as if it had happened this morning. As the teacher's hand went in the air, with every pair of eyes turned towards her, she remembers thinking, "Oh please not me. Don't do this to me. I love singi…"

The hand came down and Sue, now in her fifties, has not sung since. When there is a karaoke in the bar and the file of songs is passed around (and I've claimed Van Morrisson's *Brown-eyed Girl* for me), a voice in Sue's head plays a script more than 50 years old. It reminds her that she cannot sing. And the script paints a vivid picture in her head of her standing on the stage singing, while everyone in the audience laughs mockingly. "Don't do this to yourself Sue," it seems to whisper, deep in her subconscious, "follow me." And she dutifully obeys the voice, finding a reason to leave the room. And whom does she find outside the room? All those others who can't sing – or, more accurately, believe that they can't. Just as the fleas in the jar, the tethered elephants in India and the bear in San Diego zoo, the influence of the script prevails and the power of belief holds sway, however far from the truth it may be. Magic-weavers appreciate and understand the power and influence they can hold over young people. They work hard not to underestimate, trivialise or abuse that responsibility.

"Tread softly for you tread on my dreams."

W.B. Yeats

Some teachers understand this power and others don't. I once shadowed a group of boys around a school. Frank, the boy to whom I would be attached, was not too pleased. So when I met him on the street outside the school he responded to my cheery hello with a teenage grunt. The other boys in Frank's gang seemed to have disowned him but walked a safe distance behind as his insurance policy.

As we approached the school gate a teacher on duty was shouting: "Come on, don't be late. Get a move on!"

"What is he shouting at?" I asked Frank, "we're on time. I wonder what he's like with those who are really late?"

"Don't mind him," said Frank ruefully, "he's a shouter."

"He's not," came a voice from the group behind, "he's a dickhead."

When I ignored the comment (obeying a key rule in shadowing to stay in role) it acted as a kind of rite of passage. Seemingly, my refusal to play the adult and object to their small gesture of defiance had won me membership of the group and now I belonged. The gang began to catch up, asking questions about me, the day and what I was looking for. I observed through the day, as the lessons changed, how the key question was not 'What have we got next?' but 'Who have we got next?' An important message to all teachers.

At break-time on that day, Frank's tutor reminded him that he had to go to see the head of year about his poor attitude.

"Do I have to, Miss? You know she hates me."

"Yes," his tutor replied firmly. "Be brave and face the music."

"OK, Miss," he conceded, "but you know it'll be a waste of time."

I asked Frank if I could come and he reluctantly agreed. When we arrived at the head of year's office she was marking some books. The door was ajar and our entry caused her to lift her head towards us. Her look was withering.

"Oh, you," she said spitting out the words. "You are a waste of space. You're rude, lazy and your attitude is pathetic. I'm just waiting for you to make one more wrong move and I will personally see to it that you are thrown out."

I found her words piercing. Curiously, Frank was grinning. What she had not understood was that her script matched perfectly that in Frank's subconscious and he had spent years at school growing comfortable with it.

"Take that stupid grin off your face and get out of my sight," she hissed, compounding the problem.

Back in the form room the tutor asked if Frank had been to see the head of year. "Yeah," he replied, "just like I said, waste of time." But it had been worse than a waste of time. The year head's lack of understanding of fundamental psychology had, in fact, strengthened the negative image Frank carried of himself and his place in school.

Fortunately, his tutor did understand. "Oh Frank, Frank, Frank, Frank, Frank, Frank," she whispered, lowering her eyes.

"What's wrong, Miss?" he asked.

"Frank," she continued, "when I look at you, I see someone who is polite, kind, a good friend, courageous, strong…" As she continued her litany I watched the boy. His eyes were tearful. Realising she was getting through to him, she pointed across the room towards an imaginary figure on which the three of us fixed our gaze.

"I don't see someone who is rude, negative and disruptive. You're not like that, Frank. Stop it, son."

"I'll try, Miss," he choked.

"Go and do your best, then," she said.

As he walked slowly away she turned to me and pointed to her eyes and whispered, "Did you see the tears of cognitive dissonance?" She knew her stuff and had skilfully placed into Frank's subconscious a very different image. He had clearly found it difficult to deal with such powerful discrepancy. "And we know what will probably happen this afternoon, don't we? He's going to try and prove me wrong. That image of the *good Frank* is not strong enough yet to compete with the other. He will default to the stronger for a while. But don't worry; I'll still be here to pick him up each time he fails. I want the good Frank, the Frank that I know, to win the day, but there aren't enough of us yet, willing to change his picture and script – but I'm working on it."

"Do you know," she concluded, "he called me the oasis in his desert the other day. Excuse me, I have to go teach."

No one that young, I thought, deserved to be that good. Magic-weaving in practice.

But not everyone understands. Just recently, I observed a physical education teacher ask a group of students to line up against a wall while he invited what were clearly the two best players to pick teams. I shuddered as I contemplated the psychological damage being visited on the last three or four to be picked.

I asked one of the boys who had been left at the wall how he felt.

"You know how I felt," he replied.

"What are we going to do about it?" I asked.

"Well, I don't know what you're going to do about it but I do know what I'm going to do. I won't be standing against this wall any more."

"What do you mean?" I asked curiously.

"Because I won't be coming to PE any more."

Preferring to climb the wall to being left standing against it humiliated, he'd balanced the odds and decided that the fear of being caught truanting from a lesson was not as great as the fear of humiliation experienced each time he was last to be picked. "No contest," he whispered ruefully.

Teachers, particularly, should never underestimate the power of their influence. A former colleague described the role as either 'dream builder' or 'dream stealer'.

"Dream stealers are those who had dreams once," he would say, "but someone stole them. So now they are going to steal yours."

He glanced around the school staffroom and nodded in the direction of one corner. "There are one or two sitting over there. Dangerous, toxic people. Shouldn't be allowed within a hundred miles of young people."

I wonder whether such individuals fully understand the psychological effect of their negativity and the damage they can do.

Their role, like that of the parent, minder, mentor and sports coach, is:

- to help the student rewrite their script;
- to enable them to paint new pictures for themselves;
- to empower them to believe in themselves; to develop their self-efficacy;
- to create the confidence to deal with setbacks while remaining hopeful and optimistic;
- to become the people both they and society needs them to be.

The emergence of new thinking in: *Every Child Matters*; *All Our Futures*; *Pupil Voice* and *Excellence and Enjoyment* nudge us towards a re-think of our moral purpose.[9] But the development of adults who understand the principles of high performance, the power of self-belief and confidence is crucial to any such thinking.

The good news is the teacher makes the difference but the bad news is the teacher makes the difference.

But just how learnable is the skill of magic-weaving?

References and notes for Chapter 4

[1] Remember this is not the real meaning of the word truth. It is not the actual truth that exists but the truth as we perceive it to be.

[2] Zander, Benjamin & Zander, Rosamund Stone (2000), *The Art of Possibility: Transforming Professional and Personal Life*. Boston, MA: Harvard Business School Publishing. You may access information online from Benjamin Zander's website: www.benjaminzander.com/board/

[3] More explanation of the 'self-talk' cycle, including information about Lou Tice, may be found at The Pacific Institute website: www.thepacificinstitute.us/v2/

[4] Refer back to Hart and Risley's research in Chapter 1, see note [25].

[5] Tice, Lou (1997), *Smart Talk For Achieving Your Potential: 5 steps to get you from here to there*. Seattle, WA: The Pacific Institute

[6] Notice the subtlety in this conversation, the coach says 'when' you get to the Olympic final, not 'if'; an example of positive script writing.

[7] Smith, Alistair and Jones, John (2010), *Winning the H-Factor*. London: Alite Publications. See also: www.alite.co.uk/

[8] Roosevelt, Eleanor (1958), *On My Own*. New York: Harper and Brothers

[9] *Every Child Matters* is the title of a shared programme of change to improve outcomes for all children and young people in England. You may explore the different strands of the programme at this website: www.dcsf.gov.uk/everychildmatters/.
All Our Futures is the title of a report to government by the National Advisory Committee on Creative and Cultural Education. You may view this report at:
www.cypni.org.uk/downloads/alloutfutures.pdf .
Pupil Voice is the title of a research paper commissioned by the Department for Children, Schools and Families. The report my be viewed at:
http://www.standards.dfes.gov.uk/research/themes/pupil_voice/comfortable/
Excellence and enjoyment: A strategy for primary schools was published by the government Department for Education and Skills in 2003. It set out the future vision for primary education that built on what had already been achieved through the national strategies. You may download the document from this website: www.nationalstrategies.standards.dcsf.gov.uk/node/85063

Chapter Five

The power of synchronicity

What magic-weavers believe • What magic-weavers say • What magic-weavers do

What magic-weavers believe

In analysing the evidence of my research, I was searching for what it was that characterised magic-weavers. Was there a key feature, a particular style, or simply a random combination of behaviours that weaved the magic? I found that there are many common traits, but I have reduced them down to ten key, generic principles. The number ten yields biblical power, but I resisted the temptation to call them the ten commandments of magic-weaving.

1. An individual has to know, understand, be passionate about and live their moral purpose.

It is difficult to capture why magic-weavers come through the gate each morning. The school's mission statement should go some way towards capturing the magic but it is frustrating that so many of these are high-sounding sound bites. They look good on headed notepaper, on notice boards at the school gate or on the front cover of the development plan but they often lack passion, poetry and a magic that individuals can truly buy into.

Good teachers make you work – even when you don't want to.

Here are three that I think work:

Ruffwood School

Promoting a culture of achievement

To go further than I thought
To run faster than I hoped
To reach higher than I dreamed
To become the person I need to be

At **Beaver Road** …

- *I have a chance to dream and my dreams are fostered*
- *I have many chances to showcase my talents*
- *I am encouraged to understand my emotions and manage them*
- *I am encouraged to develop my social skills and how to use them*
- *I experience the joy of discovering nature*
- *I experience the joys and wonders of Manchester and the surrounding region*
- *I am a school, national and world citizen*

At **Beaver Road** …

- *There are no invisible children*
- *All engage*
- *Many will shine*
- *Some will reach the stars*

Maghull High School

Through challenge to achievement

Through encouragement to self-belief

Through inspiration to the dream

2. All people are of equal worth and the most important person in the world is standing in front of you now.

Weavers of magic never prioritise paper over young people and do not court favourites. They excel at just being there, at being present from moment to moment and at giving the purity of their attention.

George C. Boldt was a young clerk at a small hotel in Philadelphia.[1] One cold, miserable night, while working reception, George was approached by an elderly couple desperate to book a room for the night. George apologised explaining that, because it was a busy time for conventions, all the big hotels in the area were completely full.

Disappointed, the old couple turned to go back out into the filthy night. Taking pity, George offered them the room he had been allocated by the hotel for his night shift. The couple refused his kind offer, at first, but George would have none of it, explaining that the room would be empty most of the night anyway.

The following day as the old man departed, he told George that he should be the manager of the best hotel in America. George thanked him for his compliment and was amused when the elderly man suggested that some day he might build him one.

Two years later George received a letter from the elderly man inviting him to New York City with a return travel ticket. On arrival, he was subjected to lengthy questioning by the elderly man as to his dreams and aspirations. Finally, the man took him outside to the corner of Fifth Avenue and 34th Street. Pointing to a magnificent, red-brick building towering to the sky, he said that this was the hotel he had built for George to manage. The old man's name was William Waldorf Astor and the young man was about to become the first manager of the Waldorf Astoria[2].

3. I am not here just to teach history but to teach the love of history.

Passion again. A colleague asked a young student why she had dropped history in her option choices.

"History," he pleaded, "is such a wonderful subject." He was stunned by her response.

"Well," she explained, "for two years Mrs Smith taught me history, she just forgot to teach me the love of history, so I dropped it."

I cannot help but feel that she did not drop history, she dropped Mrs Smith. Conversely, a high school student once asked a teacher, "Sir, why do I need a teacher when I have Google?" I guess the answer is the same. Google might teach you history but it is only the magic-weaver who will teach you the love of history.

4. Attitude is the key and is always a personal choice.

The American writer, Charles Swindoll, is frequently quoted for his views about attitude.[3] According to Swindoll, your attitude has a greater impact on your life than anything else. He claims it is more important than: education, your past experiences, how much money you have, your successes and your failures, or whatever other people may do, think and say about you. It is more important than your gifts and talents or what you look like. Furthermore, it can make, or break, a business or a family.

Everyday we have the amazing ability to choose which attitude we will take up for the day. Although we can't change how other people will act, nor change what we have done in the past, we can change our attitude.

For Swindoll, life is 10% about what happens to him and 90% how he reacts to it.

And it's the same for all of us, we can control our attitudes and, through that, our destiny.

In *Man's Search for Meaning*, his moving account of life as a young man in Auschwitz, Victor Frankl explored the notion of attitude.

The horror of a concentration camp is almost unimaginable. To be dragged from a train, have your treasured personal possessions snatched away, to be marched with your family in single file through a gate where a German officer stands, his left hand supporting his right elbow, nonchalantly waving people one way and the other, to the workshop or to the gas chamber. One can only surmise that the man was perhaps enjoying separating husbands and wives, brothers from sisters and mothers from their children; even, on occasions, making a mother choose which child went which way. A scene played out so graphically in the film *Sophie's Choice*.

How could anyone be anything but a poverty thinker in that horror? Not so, Frankl claims. It was the possibility thinkers who survived the experience best and helped others survive. He notes that everyone who survived the concentration camps always remember those individuals who walked through the huts comforting other people.

These were people who would give away their last piece of food to someone else.

Frankl tells us that while there were few people like this, they did exist. This fact alone offers proof to us all that while everything can be taken away from a person and although we may be subject to horrors so despicably bad, there is one thing that cannot be taken from us – our attitude. This is the last of our freedoms. The ability to choose our own attitude in any set of circumstances, the overwhelming power to find our own way.

The Nazis could take almost everything – their family, the fillings from their teeth, the hair from their head, their life even – but there was one thing they could not take, their attitude.

Attitude is always a personal choice and should never, if negative, be blamed on anyone or anything else.

5. Children will forget what we made them think, but never how we made them feel.

Life is building memories, good and bad, and one day that is all that most of us will have left. Time at school is an important part of that memory bank. To be effective, learning has to be emotional. If not, it becomes a chore to be carried out or medicine to take in the hope that some day you will reap its benefits. Research suggests that most of what we learn at school is forgotten in adulthood. Indeed, according to the research of Ebbinghaus most of it is forgotten a few days later.[4]

I often meet former students and they want to talk about that trip, that football match, that school production. It is ironic that such crucial experiences are often confined to that most dubious of groups *extra-curricular activity*. The term itself was created decades ago in the private fee-paying world of education. It denoted those activities not included in the fees but for which parents had to pay extra.

This unfortunate differentiation has relegated such activity to a less important level. But it is the sum of the learning both formal and informal, which leaves an indelible mark on the learner. Examine an extra-curricular activity programme and you are sure to find some magic-weavers. Mick Waters describes how schooling is a blend of different yet equally valuable learning experiences.[5] Learning in lessons is important yet sits alongside learning outside of lessons (traditional extra-curricular activity), learning through the routines (assemblies, dining, visits to the toilet and changing for PE) and learning outside of school.

6. The balance of maintenance and development in life is crucial to fulfilling potential; true learning and living exists in the world of development and risk, at the edge of your comfort zone.

Being and feeling challenged is crucial to the learning process. David Hopkins' work in the area of what he calls adventure learning places the facing, tackling and overcoming of a challenge at the centre of learning and personal development.[6]

Classrooms are by their nature challenging places and simply raising a hand to answer a question can be a risky business. The culture of a classroom needs, therefore, to be in the hands of an individual who understands what Schiller meant when he wrote that children will not give the adult permission to take them to places where they cannot go on their own unless they have connected emotionally and feel safe.[7] As a result, such teachers are adept at establishing praise, and not blame, cultures.

Barbara Fredrickson's work on positivity/negativity ratios stresses the importance of a balance tipped in favour of the positive.[8] In good relationships she describes a balance of 4.5 to 1 positive to negative interactions. In dysfunctional relationships this ratio can drop to 1 to 1. Her work supports the notion that students in a positive mood state will improve their ability to be creative, problem-solve and achieve by up to 35%. Risk-taking in a supportive, collaborative context is at the core of magic-weaving.

Classrooms can be centres of adventure and challenge yet still be free of put-downs and what Pink Floyd called *dark sarcasm*. In the hands of a trusted coach, students are more likely to give the adult permission to take them to places where they cannot go alone. But that permission is predicated on trust, respect and mutual co-operation. Indeed, in their work to develop alternative approaches to teaching and learning in Limerick, colleagues recorded a strong sense among the students of not wanting to let the teacher down.[9] David Aspey, using research data on more than 10,000 students, concluded that the interpersonal skills of teachers dramatically influence the learning and mental health of young people.[10] *Caveat Terminator*.

7. The biggest influence on another's behaviour is my behaviour.

In my 17 years as a headteacher, I had to deal with numerous, difficult situations which had arisen as the result of the misbehaviour of a student. The fall-out from such situations can be widespread and the consequences traumatic for all involved. Each time I would carefully trace the incident back to find a cause. In most cases, I would unearth a trivial misdemeanour at the outset which had been escalated into a serious situation.

Most incidents in classrooms have nothing personally to do with the teacher but if the latter takes the issue personally it can rapidly become 100% to do with that adult. The irony of situations where an adult shouts at a pupil for raising her voice was never lost on me but often seemed not to register with that adult.

I learned from colleagues in the forces, the police and those involved in stewarding large public events that if an individual in control wants to be part of the solution to a potential incident and not part of the problem itself, they have to resist the sometimes irresistible urge to mimic the very behaviour that is causing concern. A natural, reptilian, threat response to be bigger, look fiercer and shout louder.

The ability to be an actor, not a reactor, involves modelling the behaviour you desire from another, not copying it. It is what I call the theory of opposites. If they shout, you speak quietly; if they snarl, you smile; if they criticise, you resist judging; if they become argumentative, you become conciliatory. More often than not I would find that magic-weavers had the ability to diffuse and de-escalate while others provoked and inflamed.

When I was a headteacher I encouraged the use of a *timeout room* where students could be sent when a conflict situation was in danger of escalating. Each year we examined detailed data of which children had been sent, the proportion of boys to girls, which year groups, what particular time of the day and, most pertinently, which staff had sent most children. Invariably, 30–40% of staff had never sent a child to the room and 20% of teachers were responsible for 80% of the referrals. Vilfredo Pareto's principle in action.[11]

8. The problem is the problem, not the child. Our mental model of that child may be the barrier to their success.

In his best-selling book, *The Fifth Discipline*, Peter Senge describes five key disciplines of a learning organisation.[12] Understanding the power of our mental models, the third key discipline, is important in knowing how they shape our view of the world and the people in it.

Put simply, mental models are an internal symbol of external reality. They are a kind of time-saving, shortcut to comprehending the complex world around us and making decisions accordingly. They are, therefore, by nature incomplete, limited by their simplicity, selective in their use of data and based on past assumptions. In the world of human interaction, such as a classroom, they can be dangerous.

Staff can meet a new student who appears *tabula rasa* before them.[13] However, on hearing the student's name, it is difficult not to recoil at the memory of that child's deviant brother and judge her accordingly. The names of certain families and individuals often circulate the staffroom, forming mental models or reputations, earned or unearned, in the minds of those staff who may have not even met that child yet. Labelling in this way, while understandable in human terms, is dangerous and can be toxic. The ability to see not a problem child but simply a child who has a problem is a key skill.

9. Those who need our support the most will
    probably deserve it the least.

Alan Blankstein, the author of *Failure is not an
Option*, once told me the story of a teacher who
offered her hand to one of her more challenging
students as he entered the classroom each day.[14] Each
day the student refused to take it until, after two or
three weeks the teacher, as he entered the room, put
her hand behind her back. The boy stopped, stared
and asked her why she had done that.

"Done what?" the teacher replied.

"Put your hand behind your back like that."

"Well," the young woman replied, "I have offered
you my hand for a few weeks now and you always
refuse it."

"That's as maybe," came the response, "but I didn't
think you'd give up so easily on me." He may not
have taken the hand but he needed to see it there.

Jean Rudduck and Julia Flutter describe a debate
which all schools should have to discover the simple
answer to the question:[15]

What kind of young people do we want today?

They divide young people into four groups:

passive positive (accepting)	active positive (influencing)
passive negative (indifferent)	active negative (rejecting)

Many teachers are honest enough to admit that working in a school where the predominant group is passive positive is a pleasure. The pupils attend regularly, quite like school and teachers, do what they are told and trust school to deliver them a future.

However, if schools fill the streets of their communities with passive positive citizens we are all in trouble. The potential for exploitation and unchallenged injustice will be high.

On the other hand, active positive students can exert great influence. They want to talk to teachers about their progress, they discuss problems they face, take responsibility, organise things and are ready to help others.

Passive negative students tend to mistrust school and teachers, will not engage with support, will follow the active negative group and will deny any concern about their lack of progress.

The active negative group will engage in anti-social behaviour, refuse to accept codes of conduct, attend irregularly, frequently find themselves on report and face the almost daily threat of exclusion.

Both negative categories will be more likely to come from low income families with little support and live in poor neighbourhoods.[16] They will experience 600 to 1200 words an hour compared to 2300 words an hour experienced by children from more affluent families.[17] Their negativity to positivity ratios will be high (more discouragement than encouragement) and they will have developed learned helplessness but, more importantly, learned hopelessness. There is much work to be done with these negative groups.

William Sanders and June Rivers researched the effect that ineffective teachers can have.[18] Their conclusions were stark. If a student has an ineffective teacher for one year, it will take two years with an effective teacher for the student to catch up. After two consecutive years with ineffective teachers, a student may never catch up. Most startlingly, a poor student is five times more likely to have an inexperienced or inadequately trained teacher.

Schools can and do make the difference, but it is particularly in work with the negative student groups that most gains can be made as long as teachers refuse to accept what can be sustained rejection. Schools must be prepared to:

- rethink the way they do business;
- accept that demographics does not have to equal destiny;
- fight to combat hopelessness; and
- instil in all their children the self-confidence to believe that they can and will succeed.

Bob Barr and Bill Parrett are under no illusion that what children, particularly those who are most at risk, need is a caring relationship with an adult.[19] These students need to see the system offer its hand of support and care on a day-to-day basis even though they may appear to not want to take it.

10. They will be smart enough if we are good enough. Never throw away your L-plates.

Socrates once pronounced that he was the wisest man in Athens because he was the only one who really knew how much he did not know.[20]

The tenth principle nails the notion that it is the staff, the guardians of the system, who have to be constantly alert to the fact that if the children are not responding or engaging in what we do, then we have to change what we do and the way we do it.

Those schools and staff who point the finger of blame at: the children *kids these days*, the local community *kids from around here* or society in general *the good old days*, miss the point.

In a changing world, Darwin claimed, it is the not the most intelligent who survive but those who are most adaptable to change. The endless journey to be good enough requires of an individual: humility, hope, courage and an enormous capacity to learn and grow. They ask not what their country can do for them but what they can do for their country, using President John F. Kennedy's famous saying.

I once visited a classroom and the teacher was complaining that she had been through an explanation four times "… and they still don't understand it. What is wrong with this class?"

Eric Hoffer, the American philosopher, reminds us that in a changing world, it is the learners who will adapt while those who think they know it all will find themselves perfectly suited to a world that no longer exists.

I bit my tongue, resisting the urge to suggest that the problem might not be the students but her explanation. And those students were smart. She had explained how the boys in ancient Rome were so athletic that every morning they would swim across the River Tiber three times before breakfast. Unimpressed, one boy retorted that they may have been athletic but they were very stupid. The teacher looked puzzled.

"If you swim across a river three times," he explained, "you finish up on the opposite side to your clothes."

And what about these from school tests:

Q: Name a bird that cannot fly
A: A roast chicken.

I would have left it blank.

The teacher could not mark this correct but gave it a mark for creativity:

Q: Name the mythological creature that was half man and half beast
A: Buffalo Bill

I have not listed an eleventh principle but if I had it would be this: magic-weavers have a great sense of humour and never, ever, take themselves too seriously.

The words that teachers use with their students are clues to their fundamental beliefs. Listen to a magic-weaver talking to students and you will learn how to develop mutual respect.[21] Here is an acronym that provides some insights:[22]

What magic-weavers say

*R*eassuring: *'I know you thought this would be a good way of doing this and…'*
*E*nthusiastic: *'I really like the way you…'*
*S*teady: *'That's OK. I'll wait while you pick them all up again.'*
*P*ractical: *'Let's see what happens when we try this again…'*
*E*ngaging: *'I'll do it first, then you try.'*
*C*lear: *'When you move your hand more slowly, you will stop smudging your writing.'*
*T*ruthful: *'You're not as good kicking with your left foot as your right, so we should practise.'*

In addition, I offer a list of the kind of phrases, often used instinctively, that I have heard magic-weavers use. Others might find them useful, whatever their role. Here are ten to try.

1. *'What I like about you is…'*

I took the first from a teacher who systematically used it with two or three students each day (often those he did not know well). After the first month of doing it one of the students said, "What I like about you is you're always saying 'what I like about you is…'" The student had learned the script.

2. *'When I look at you I see someone who…'*

The second phrase is a skilful way of delivering a

> "Education is a conversation between one generation and another about the things which are important."
>
> Bart McGettrick

negative message while leaving the self-esteem of the individual intact. It takes resolve for an adult to stay calm and praise a student who has just done something silly or annoying, but believe me it works. It is difficult to resist listing the misdemeanours and ripping into the individual in the heat of the interaction but delivering a dose of praise before the bad news is effective. If followed then by 'I don't see someone who…' before describing the offence and concluding with: 'You are not like that, John, stop it.' This skill can yield surprising results.

Put another way, you have just criticised the act, not the child, and have turned what could be a negative scriptwriting moment into a more positive experience for both of you. And you still got the message across.

3. *'Have I explained that clearly?'*

Using phrases such as this, the teacher draws the focus of the attention away from the inadequacies of the learner (Do you understand?) and on to the performance of the instructor. I remember hearing a teacher explain to her students that a red mark on a piece of work did not mean the student had made a mistake, but rather that she (the teacher) had not explained it properly.

4. *'That's not like you, the next time…' or 'You're so much better than that.'*

Two phrases which create a positive script even after someone has done something wrong. Compare with such alternatives as: 'That is so typical of you' or 'You're such a rude person.'

In England, putting students *on report* is a common behaviour modification strategy for those whose conduct has not been good enough. Teachers have to sign the card at the end of every lesson ticking which of the behaviour targets that individual has met successfully. Ian Gilbert tells the tale of a teacher who, when students arrived in his lesson with a report card, always signed it at the start of the lesson 'Brilliant'.[23] He never, he claimed, had to change the judgement.

5. *'What can I do to help you learn more?'*

A reflective question which, in the right context can effectively engage the student in the development of their own learning. It may empower the student by not only encouraging them to have a better understanding about the right learning conditions for them but also enables the teacher to move towards personalising their approach to each individual child. It is a short step to the corollary question: 'In what ways could your behaviour help me teach you better?'

6. *'How do you feel about that?'*

During lessons teachers often seek the thoughts of their students when it can be more useful and appropriate to enquire about how they feel. Feelings and not just thoughts are a key determinant as to whether a task set will be completed successfully or not.

7. *'When you behave like that, I feel...'*

This kind of statement is useful as a way of commenting on good or poor behaviour. It can nudge the other person towards a sense of responsibility for their actions and away from a preoccupation with how they are feeling. It can promote empathy and, coupled with the skilful use of an Agreement Frame, it can be a good behaviour modification tool.[24] An Agreement Frame occurs when you say:

- What you can see to be true.
- What you know to be true.
- What you believe to be true.
- What is compatible with how you are feeling.

It makes it easier to encourage agreement with phrases such as: 'Thank you for staying so calm. I can understand why you are upset at what Mr Smith has said to you.'

8. *Describing behaviour, not judging or trying to control it.*

When someone raises their voice, 'You're shouting' is more likely to draw a positive response than 'Shut up' or 'You are such a noisy person'. When someone is emotionally upset, 'You're crying' may be a more sensitive response than 'What's wrong?' They may be tears of joy.

9. *Replacing 'don't' with 'be'.*

The words 'don't' invite resistance (ask any parent) and the brain finds it difficult to negate a negative. Faced with a difficult shot over a lake, when the golfer whispers to herself, 'Don't go in the lake' her brain is actually instructing her body to do precisely that.

The parent who says to a child, 'Don't go on the road you'll get killed,' is planting the wrong script and picture into the subconscious with negative goal-setting. An alternative, such as 'Be safe, stay on the pavement' is a healthier instruction in the same way that, 'Be respectful and speak quietly, thank you' is likely to achieve a better response than: ' Don't bug people and don't shout out, you noisy boy!'

10. *'I saw this and I thought of you.'*

Naturally, you have to be careful what you saw.

One of my favourite stories is of a teacher who had a boy in her class whom she described as the grit in her oyster; the demon who visited her in her mind at 3am, when she knew she had to teach him the following morning. She discovered he was passionate about fishing and one weekend, while buying herself a magazine, she saw one on fishing and bought it. Passing the boy on the corridor the next day, she gave him the magazine.

"I saw this and thought of you," she explained. The boy was shocked.

"Er, thanks, I'll bring it back after school."

"That's OK, it's yours."

"I'll bring the money for it in tomorrow," he stuttered.

"No need. It's a gift."

Later that day, during the lesson, he asked if she liked fishing. "Of course," she lied and went straight to the library after class to borrow a book on fishing. Fishing had created an emotional connection and, strangely, his behaviour started to improve.

The teacher learned that he fished in competitions on the canal bank each Friday evening. One Friday she was going to dinner with her husband and, passing over the canal bridge, she shouted, "Stop the car. I want to go and see how he is doing."

As her husband grumbled about being late, she tottered down the canal's cinder path and caught sight of him in the middle of a long row of float-focussed fishermen. As she approached he looked up.

"Hiya, Miss. Wow! You look the business."

"Thanks," she replied. "I've just come to see how you're getting on."

Lifting his keep-net which teemed with fish, he said, "Great, I think I'm going to be in the money tonight."

"Wonderful," she replied, "let me know how you get on, on Monday."

As she turned to go, the boy looked up. "Miss."

"Yes," she answered.

"Thanks for coming."

She never had trouble with him again.

Thinking about the application of Daniel Goleman's ideas, I would call this emotional brilliance.[25] How many would even have known he liked fishing, bothered to learn about it, or turned up on a Friday evening?

But that's not the end of the story. Two years later, on the last day of term, as the children were leaving, some, including our fisherman, for ever, the teacher was clearing her desk for the summer break. She became aware of someone standing at the door to her room. It was him.

"I know you haven't taught me for a couple of years," he explained, "but I saw this and thought of you."

From behind his back he produced a by now tattered, well-thumbed, fishing magazine. "Thanks Miss. I'll see you around."

As he turned to go the teacher smiled. "Thanks for coming," she whispered, wiping a tear from her eye.

These are just ten. There are many, many more gems that the attentive listener can note and use. Listen for such phrases, write them down and practise them. Practice will fix them in the subconscious until they become your default setting – the way you are. A simple process of developing sound, neuro-linguistic habits.[26]

Some have a knack of speaking this way naturally. For the rest of us the skill has to be learned, but the effort will be repaid many times over in the kind of responses drawn from the listener.

From police officers and soldiers on patrol to football referees and teachers, the knowledge that the greatest influence on another's behaviour is your behaviour, will greatly determine the world we create around us. Done skilfully, the effects can be astounding.

Psychologist and organisational change consultant, Robert Gass, tells us that what we see and hear affects what we think about.

What we think about determines how we feel.

How we feel influences our reactions.

Our reactions become our habits which, ultimately, determine our destiny.

What magic-weavers do

Whatever their beliefs and no matter what they say, we eventually really know people through their actions. What they actually do is more important than what they say or profess to believe.

Here are some examples of behaviour that I have noted on visits to schools, or when colleagues at presentations and workshops have been invited to share instances of magic-weaving.

1. *Turn up.*

> I don't care how much you know, until I know how much you care.

- Turn up to school sports/shows – remember two things they did well.
- Let them know you are going just to see them.
- Sign up for school holidays/trips.
- Have lunch with them in their dining room and vary the table/group.

One primary head described how he had had trouble with a group of teenage youths who were continually coming on to the school site in the evenings and vandalising the school. He turned up one evening not to ask them to stop doing damage but why they were doing it. He wasn't surprised to hear the teenage refrain of nothing to do around here so he asked what he could do to help.

"Will you let us play football here?" they asked.

"I'll do better than that," he said, "I'll coach you and if you're any good we'll form a team, buy some kit and enter a league. Are you up for it?"

The vandalising ceased and when one of the young men died tragically the following year the head was invited to the funeral. He cried when the boy's mother told him that her son would be buried in the football strip. It was, she explained, the one real positive thing in her son's life.

2. *Know their identity.*

A colleague told how she learned and noted down in her *identity diary* three school and three personal things about each student she taught. It had such a positive impact that she now does the same for everyone she meets. The effect is amazing, she recalled.

Another described her *achievement wall.*

"What is that?" I enquired.

"Well," she replied, "everyone in my class is better than I am at something. I find out what it is and we put names in the bricks on the wall together with the area of expertise. We have everything from fishing and French to maths and making the evening meal. If you want help with any area you don't come to me you go to the expert. I try to ensure that each area of expertise is covered in the curriculum at least once per term and it is the expert, not me, who leads the sessions."

"Are you up there?" I asked.

"Yes, that's me," she laughed, "horse-riding."

3. *Remember them.*

Remember their name or nickname (if it's positive). My colleague Alistair Smith often says that it is easier to de-motivate than motivate and the easiest way to de-motivate someone is to forget their name.

One secondary school produces a newsletter each term (semester) and the editor's main responsibility is to ensure that as many student names as possible appear in print. In brackets, after the name, they list the primary school that student attended. The primary teachers recorded how the idea made the document come alive. In particular the *Where are they now?* Alumni page.

The same high school, after the publication of the examination achievements of its students, writes to thank each primary school individually for the role it had to play in the success of its students. It also lists their university/college/career destination and regularly updates the list.

4. *Believe in them.*

Balance praise with criticism. One teacher had what she described as an *appreciation strategy* where she consciously recorded, particularly with her more challenging students, the number of times she had been critical with the number of times she had said *well done* and *that's great*. She understood the power of positivity ratios.

Another described how she wrote a personal letter to each of her students just before their public examinations. In the letter she recalled:

- why it had been good to have that individual in the group,
- what they had contributed, and
- her confidence in their ability to succeed.

It had taken time, she explained, but the number of students who, even years later recalled, and even produced, that letter made it worth the effort.

5. *Catch them winning.*

Spot ordinary things done extraordinarily well. Here are a baker's dozen ordinary things to spot and praise:

- Being on time
- Sitting
- Listening
- Working in a team
- Smiling
- Contributing
- Helping
- Being patient
- Putting hand in the air
- Bringing equipment
- Looking smart
- Having a sense of humour
- Staying calm

Capping the praise with something like: 'That's just what I'm looking for, Mary, brilliant' can have extraordinary power not only to diffuse a situation but to create the likelihood of a positive response.

6. *Make lessons worthy of the students' good behaviour.*

My friend Alan Boyle visited a fish restaurant in Boston and was intrigued to find at his setting the following pledge made by the restaurant management to its customers:[27]

> *We Pledge:*
>
> *To inspect and prepare the freshest, highest quality fish and shellfish*
> *To assure you of a clean and comfortable environment*

*To promote diversity and respect for all
human differences
To provide prompt, friendly, and courteous
service by a knowledgeable and highly-
trained staff
To be sensitive to special dietary needs and
provide a list of ingredients upon request
To deliver all foods and beverages, prepared
to guest satisfaction, in a timely and efficient
manner
To feature a wine list that represents the best
overall value in America
To respond in a rapid, sensitive and non-
confrontational manner to requests that will
enhance your dining experience
To provide you with an experience that will
encourage you to return*

It struck him that it was as refreshing as it was reassuring that the staff were there to ensure a high quality experience.

During his meal he pondered about the different type of pledges and behaviour codes that he was more familiar with, pinned up in classrooms. It is perhaps ironic that in many classrooms it appears to be the students (the consumers) who have to make the pledge to the staff (the teacher), sometimes, sadly, regardless of the quality of teaching.

Many schools have righted this and have guaranteed a high quality experience for its students whatever classroom or subject they happen to experience. They make it explicit in contracts and charters and so feel comfortable drawing up *if I … then you* contracts and agreements.

7. Create 'I can' classrooms.

In their book *Teacher Talk*, Nancy and Chick Moorman tell the story of fourth grade teacher, Donna.

One day Donna asked her class to write on a blank piece of paper, entitled 'I Can't', all the things they couldn't do.[28]

There was no problem listing things that couldn't be done, such as: 'I can't run as fast as Jim', 'I can't do fractions', 'I can't get Anna to like me'.

Donna, the teacher, also wrote her list: 'I can't get Robert to sit still all lesson', 'I can't meet Lucy's parents to talk about her progress'.

Next, Donna collected all the slips of paper and put them into an empty cardboard box. After sealing the lid with tape, she took her class outside to the garden just below their classroom window.

Then she got the children to dig a hole deep enough to bury the box. After placing the box in the hole, she gathered the class in a circle around the box and made an homily.

In her short speech, Donna said they were gathered to pay tribute to 'I Can't'. While he was alive he had touched everyone in the class and some more than others.

His influence had been felt far and wide, in schools far and wide and in every public building in the land, including the government. This was to be his final resting place. He would be heard of no more.

Donna brightened up when she said that 'I Can't' had brothers and sisters who survived. Their names are: 'I Can', 'I Will' and 'I'm Going to Right Now'.

She told the class that although they were less famous than their brother, with the help of the class they could make a bigger impact on everyone.

Donna ended her talk by wishing that 'I Can't' would rest in peace allowing everyone to pick up their lives and move on without him.

After filling in the hole the children returned to their classroom where Donna erected a plaque.

I CAN'T

MAY HE REST IN PEACE

MARCH 27, 2009

From that day, whenever one of her students said: "I can't," she would point to the plaque and exchange smiles.

8. *Champion creativity and imagination.*

At the age of six we have, in our country, the most creative children on the planet. Sir Ken Robinson, chair of the committee that produced *All Our Futures*, recalled how, during a visit to a classroom, he asked a young girl what she was doing.[29]

"I'm just drawing God," came the nonchalant reply.

"Wow!" said Sir Ken, "nobody knows what God looks like."

"Well," she replied, not bothering to raise her head from the page, "you will in a minute."

If you ask six-year-olds who can draw, as I have done on a number of occasions, every hand will probably be raised enthusiastically. Then ask 11 year olds, you will be lucky to get double figures.

What happens to that creative self-belief? The regime of testing has undoubtedly raised standards in numeracy and literacy but at what cost? Pressurised staff teaching to the test, parents increasing the pressure on staff and children to perform, children fearing to fail and schools sacrificing creative approaches for more traditional methods. Sixty per cent of the curriculum experience for Year 6 children is preparing in one way or another for the end-of-year test (SAT).

But more and more schools in England are refusing to be intimidated by the tyranny of testing and are embracing:

- a more creative approach to the curriculum; the focus on key skills;
- the re-birth of project-based learning;
- the growth of philosophical enquiry;
- values education;
- the popularity of Social and Emotional Aspects of Learning (SEAL);
- the raised status of vocational education;
- multiple intelligence approaches;
- the development of Learning to Learn methodologies.

These 'minority' areas are becoming more and more mainstream without any sudden drop in performance in tests. David Hodgson's book of inspirational teaching activities is a great place to start for anyone wondering how to let go of traditional methodology.[30]

Starting each day with one of Ian Gilbert's *Thunks* is another.[31] Try these for size:

- Is not going fishing a hobby?
- If I borrow a million pounds am I a millionaire?
- If you found a contraceptive in your child's bedroom should you be pleased?
- Is something boring because of it or because of you?
- If I read a comic in a shop without paying, is that stealing?

And here's one from me: Should you have more than one supermarket loyalty card?

It's catching.

9. *Act, not react.*

Pedro Noguera professor at New York University, tells the story of a student who put his hand up at the back of the class and proceeded to ask the teacher how many times she had had sex with her husband the previous week.[32] I would challenge most professionals not to see a win-lose situation here, but the young teacher understood the basic rule of behaviour management, to be an actor not a reactor.

She remained calm, smiled, ignored the audacity and carried on with the lesson.

But he was persistent. "Mrs Johnson," he continued, "are you ignoring me?"

"No," she replied, "I'm still counting."

Most issues in classrooms are nothing personally to do with the teacher but, once the teacher takes a misdemeanour personally, now it's all about the teacher.

Bill Rogers[33] and Andy Vass[34] describe a series of effective techniques which can move the teacher in to active not reactive mode. Gary Wilson draws from the work of Rogers and Vass and cites examples of such strategies he has observed or helped develop in the schools with whom he works.[35] Here are three typical techniques that they advocate.

Repetition (Broken record): Calmly repeating a request, with the same voice and tone, until the student complies.

Buying time (Passing technique): Avoid confrontation when somebody arrives late for class. No need to waste everyone else's time. Smile and say, 'Good to see you; find a seat and we'll talk about it later.'

Assertive request (Reinforcing frame): Often, the simplest strategy is the most powerful. When you ask a student to do something, say *thank you* instead of saying *please*. The word *please* suggests that the student has a choice about whether to comply or not. Using *thank you* instead is more assertive in terms of behaviour management. This implies that the student is expected to follow without any choice in the matter. 'Put your bag under the table, Jasmine, thank you.'

10. *Like children and have fun.*

William Fry, a psychiatrist at Stanford Medical School, found that, on average, children laugh about three to four times more per day than adults.[36] Other findings vary the figure, but what is indisputable is that young people let their faces know that they are having a good time far more often than we adults.

I like children – I just couldn't eat a full one.

Freddie Starr

As a headteacher, I used to put at the top of the essential characteristics list for job applications to the school – 'Likes children'.

In recent years, the figure for those leaving the profession prematurely has risen and excessive workload is often cited as the key reason. That may be what finally tips the balance, but, and it is just my opinion, based on 17 years as a headteacher, the tipping of that scale was the result of a sustained period of losing emotional connectedness with young people, with their manner, their moods and their music. Gladys Knight once sang 'I would rather live in his world than live without him in mine.' It is those staff who engage with the world of young people (or at least meet them half way) who seem to relate to them best.

"I always try to have a good day," one teacher told me, "even when I'm not feeling so positive. It's what I'm paid to do, but more important, what I want to do. And, however down I may be feeling, it is amazing how young people have the ability to rescue my day."

Bart McGettrick summed it up when he said that the key to behaviour management and, I would argue, to unlocking their world, lies in the smiling eyes of the teacher.[37]

References and notes for Chapter 5

[1] George C. Boldt arrived in America, with little money, in the 1860s and became a self-made millionaire.

[2] The story of George Boldt and the Waldorf Astoria is adapted from: Hedges, Burke (1996), *You, Inc., Vol1: Discover the C.E.O. within.* Sisters, OR: International Network Training Institute Publishing & Resource Books Inc. Another version of this story is available on the web at: www.snopes.com/glurge/waldorf.asp (This version corrects some of the embellishments in the more popular story).

[3] Swindoll, Charles R. (2006), *Great Attitudes: 10 Choices for Success in Life.* Nashville, TN: J. Countryman. Read his famous quote on attitude here: www.bigeye.com/attitude.htm

[4] Ebbinghaus, Hermann (1913), *Memory: A Contribution to Experimental Psychology.* New York: Teachers College. This was the translation of Ebbinghaus's original text published in 1885. Here is a weblink to an online version of the original translation: www.psy.ed.asu.edu/~classics/Ebbinghaus/index.htm

[5] Mick Waters is the former director of curriculum at the Qualifications and Curriculum Authority (QCA) for England.

[6] Hopkins, David and Putnam, Roger (1993), *Personal Growth Through Adventure.* Abingdon: David Fulton.

[7] Schiller, J.C. Friedrich von (1794), *Letters Upon the Aesthetic Education of Man.* A pdf of the translation into English may be found at this link: www.filepedia.org/files/Letters%20Upon%20The%20Aesthetic%20Education%20of%20Man.pdf

[8] Fredrickson, Barbara (2009), *Positivity.* New York: Crown.

[9] Looney, Anne (2008), presentation at Quest Conference, York Region District School Board, Ontario. Anne is chief executive of the National Council for Curriculum and Assessment for Ireland.

[10] Aspey, David and Roebuck, F (1977), *Kids Don't Learn From People They Don't Like.* Amhurst, MA: Human Resource Development Press.

[11] The Pareto principle is more generally known as the 80:20 rule. It was first noted by Pareto in 1906 that 80% of the land in Italy was owned by 20% of the population. A translation of Pareto's initial observations was published: Pareto, Vilfredo and Page, Alfred N. (1971), *Manual of Political Economy.* New York: A.M. Kelley. Since then, the 80:20 rule has been applied to many situations in business and the workplace.

[12] Senge, Peter (1990), *The Fifth Discipline: The Art and Practice of the Learning Organisation*. New York: Doubleday/Currency. Senge's five key disciplines are: Systems thinking; Personal mastery; Mental models; Building shared vision and Team learning.

[13] Like a blank slate.

[14] Blankstein, Alan M. (2004), *Failure is Not an Option: Six principles that guide student achievement in high-performing schools*. Thousand Oaks, CA: Corwin.

[15] Rudduck, Jean and Flutter, Julia (2004), *Consulting Pupils: What's in it for schools?* London: Routledge Falmer.

[16] Bracey, G. W. (2002), Raising achievement of at-risk students – or not. In *Phi Delta Kappan* 83 (6), pp431–432.

[17] Refer back to Hart and Risley's research in Chapter 1; see Chapter 1 note [27].

[18] Sanders, William L. and Rivers, June C. (1996), *Cumulative and residual effects of teachers on future student academic achievement*. Knoxville, TN: University of Tennessee, Value-Added Research and Assessment Center.

[19] Barr, Robert D. and Parrett, William H. (2007), *The Kids Left Behind: Catching Up the Underachieving Children of Poverty*. Bloomington, IN: Solution Tree. This important book presents a synthesis of research across the United States on what works in high-performing, high-poverty schools.

[20] The wisdom of not knowing is dealt with in this text: Philips, Christopher (2002), *Socrates Café: A Fresh Taste of Philosophy*. New York: W.W. Norton & Co Inc.

[21] Lawrence-Lightfoot, Sara (2000), *Respect: An Exploration*. Cambridge, MA: Perseus Books. This stunning book analyses the most powerful ingredient in any relationship. The author is professor at Harvard University School of Education.

[22] Smith, Alistair and Lucas, Bill (2002), *Help Your Child to Succeed: The Essential Guide for Parents* Stafford: Network Educational Press.

[23] Gilbert, Ian (2002), *Essential Motivation in the Classroom*. London: RoutledgeFalmer.

[24] For further information about Agreement Frames, see: Wilson, Gary (2006), *Breaking Through Barriers to Boys' Achievement: Developing a caring masculinity*. London: Network Continuum Education.

[25] Goleman, Daniel (2000), *Working with Emotional Intelligence*. New York: Bantam Books.

[26] To learn more about neuro-linguistic programming, try this website: www.nwnlp.com/nlp.html

[27] Legal Sea Foods has a chain of restaurants along the eastern coast of USA. The pledge is inscribed on a placemat presented to each customer.

[28] Moorman, Chick and Moorman-Weber, Nancy (1989), *Teacher Talk: What it Really Means*. Merrill, MI: Personal Power Press.

[29] Robinson, Ken (2001), *Out of Our Minds: Learning to be Creative*. Oxford: Capstone Publishing. Professor Sir Ken Robinson was the chair of the National Advisory Committee on Creative and Cultural Education. The committee was established in 1998 by David Blunkett when he was secretary of state for education. The committee's report *All Our Futures: Creativity, Culture and Education* was published in 1999. The report may be viewed online via this link: www.cypni.org.uk/downloads/alloutfutures.pdf

[30] Hodgson, David (2009), *The Little Book of Inspirational Teaching Activities: Bringing NLP into the classroom*. Carmarthen: Crown House Publishing.

[31] Gilbert, Ian (2008), *The Little Book of Thunks: 260 questions to make your brain go ouch!* Carmarthen: Crown House Publishing.

[32] A list of articles published by Pedro Noguero appears on his In Motion Magazine via this link www.inmotionmagazine.com/noguera.html

[33] Rogers, Bill (2009), *How to Manage Children's Challenging Behaviour (Second Edition)*. London: Paul Chapman Publishing.

[34] Hook, Peter and Vass, Andy (2004), *Behaviour Management Pocketbook*. Alresford, Hampshire: Teachers Pocketbooks.

[35] Wilson, Gary (2006), *Breaking Through Barriers to Boys' Achievement: Developing a caring masculinity*. London: Network Continuum Education.

[36] Fry, William and Salameh, W. (Eds) (1987), *Handbook of humour and psychotherapy: Advances in the clinical use of humour*. Sarasota, FL: Professional Resources Exchange Inc.

[37] Professor Bart McGettrick is dean of education at Liverpool Hope University. He gave his inaugural lecture on 30 January 2008.

Chapter Six

To serve them all my days

The magic of John Keating • Returning the profession to professionals • A pedagogy of justice

The magic of John Keating

In 1989 Peter Weir directed the film *Dead Poet's Society* set in Welton Academy, Vermont, a traditional, conservative boys' prep school. Welton aspires to four principles: tradition, honour, discipline and excellence. The film tells the story of an English teacher, John Keating (played by Robin Williams), who encourages his students to break the bonds of conformity and think for themselves. He invites his students to call him Mr Keating or, if they are feeling a little more daring, *O Captain! My Captain*, the title of a Walt Whitman poem.

In his first lesson, whistling the *1812 Overture*, he leads the boys to the school museum. Perusing old photographs of former Welton students, he challenges the boys to seize the day, *carpe diem*.

In another lesson, he invites one of them to read the introduction to a fictional work *Understanding Poetry* by Dr J. Evans Pritchard. The author claims that to fully understand poetry you must measure its score for structural perfection on the horizontal of a graph and plot its importance on the vertical. Calculating the total area of a poem becomes relatively easy, thus enabling the reader to measure its greatness.

Keating describes the introduction as excrement and, to the immortal line of: "Be gone J. Evans Pritchard PhD," invites his incredulous students to rip out the entire introduction. "I want to hear nothing but the ripping of Dr Pritchard."

Encouraging the boys to be individuals, he instructs them to stand on their desks in order to see the world from another perspective. He implores them in what could be a timeless anthem for teaching.

He warns his students that they are about to engage in battle in an intellectual war for the sake of their hearts and souls. They are going to resist the armies of academics who are fighting to measure poetry in some objective manner. That must never be tolerated.

He promises the class that they will remember how to think for themselves. Then he lets them into a little secret. They will not read poetry because it is cute. Instead, they are going to read and write poetry because it stirs up passion and that is what the human race needs more than anything else.

Keating recognises the importance of noble professions such as: medicine, law, business and engineering, whilst reminding his students that the things which keep us alive are: poetry, beauty, romance and love. Then he rouses them by quoting Whitman:

O me! O life! ... of the questions of these
recurring;
Of the endless trains of the faithless - of cities
fill'd with the foolish;

...

The question, O me! so sad, recurring -
What good amid these, O me, O life?

Answer.
That you are here - that life exists, and
identity;
That the powerful play goes on, and you may
contribute a verse.

Keating concludes with a powerful question to each of his students: "What will your verse be?"

What I find compelling about the film is that Thomas Schulman, the author, found the inspiration for the character of John Keating in his former English teacher at Montgomery Bell Academy, Samuel F. Pickering Jr. Interestingly, Robin Williams partly based his character on John C. Campbell, his history teacher at Detroit Country Day School. Two great teachers who had left an indelible mark on the lives of both men.

In the film's powerful denouement, Keating is dismissed from his classroom by headmaster Gale Nolan. But to the latter's fury, one by one Keating's students stand on their desks bidding him farewell with Whitman's refrain, *O Captain! My Captain!*

There are messages here for the profession today. The traditional world of prep schooling confronted by John Keating saw him as an outcast, a rebel and exception to the rule. Such powerful norms, often lying unquestioned and unchallenged for decades, shape culture and determine the way we do things around here.[1] Creativity, innovation and ingenuity were enemies of the state.

During the last two decades of the twentieth century there was a remarkable shift in education in the UK. Control of the curriculum was removed from schools by central government. At the same time, responsibility for standards was transferred from government to schools.

Returning the profession to professionals

Centralised control was the inevitable result of a feeling in the 1980s that schools, in general, and teachers, in particular, needed to be reined in. The teaching profession was perceived merely as a delivery mechanism for central policy reforms and initiatives, determined by others beyond the classroom and the school. The result was increased prescription, greater accountability, focused public scrutiny and a call for tighter standards.

In Model G, Sir Michael Barber graphically charts this history of educational development.[2] Encouragingly, he describes a period during which the teaching profession has moved from a position of low trust, heavy prescription and high accountability to one, at the beginning of the new millennium, where teachers and schools are being challenged to take the lead and start to think for themselves again, just as Keating's students.

	Knowledge poor		
	1980s	1970s	
	Uninformed	Uninformed	
	prescription	professional	
National		judgement	Professional
Prescription	1990s	2000s	Judgement
	Informed	Informed	
	prescription	professional	
		judgement	
	Knowledge rich		

Model G: Time map of dynamics between government and the teaching profession in England

Way back in 1960, Douglas McGregor proposed two sets of contrasting assumptions which underpin motivation in the workplace.[3]

Theory X saw people as fundamentally workshy, avoiding responsibility and unwilling to work hard, unless directed or threatened.

Theory Y, on the other hand, suggested that, under the right conditions, the average person will show imagination and ingenuity, will seek to take on responsibility and show commitment.

In Barber's time map, Theory X thinking appears to have dominated government policy in the eighties and nineties. At least two decades of centralised policy produced critics and casualties. James Flaherty suggests that such command-and-control policy has induced a kind of *learned helplessness* in the profession.[4] Andrew Fraser describes it as de-professionalisation.[5] One headteacher explained to me that he felt as if he had lived in a curriculum cage for many years and suddenly they had opened the cage door.

"Do you know what?" he admitted, ruefully, "I'm too frightened to fly out."

But the age of informed professional judgement, which acknowledges the expertise and values the views of the profession, is recognition that a time has come when the teachers can take control of their own destiny. For the new age of informed professional judgement to thrive, Andrew Fraser sees the need for what he describes as key paradigm shifts:

- from pragmatism to philosophical enquiry;
- from informed prescription to informed professional judgement;

- from a dependency culture to one based on professional authority;
- from best practice thinking (what is working now) to next practice thinking (what could work more powerfully)

In his excellent book *Coaching,* James Flaherty develops this thinking by proposing, if not a new paradigm, then a serious alternative to command-and-control thinking.

One of the key ideas that underpin Flaherty's book is the clear recognition that organisations which adopt command-and-control practices are *de facto* unable to create the conditions and develop the necessary competencies that would enable them to successfully meet their challenges in the twenty-first century.

The reason for this is rooted in the beliefs and values that characterise command-and-control organisations. The fundamental belief is that the most effective way to structure the organisation is through a power and knowledge hierarchy with those at the top controlling both. This is because most people who work in the organisation are not trusted. A small number of people at the top make all the decisions and these are implemented through the hierarchy. Everyone is closely monitored to ensure they comply with prescribed actions. Organisations like this are expensive to run, slow to function and they are doomed in a rapidly changing world.

Flaherty accepts he is neither the first nor the only person to make such an observation; far from it. But he needs to register these limitations as the premise for his alternative way of working. His ideas stem from the belief that organisations should operate in ways that empower people to be both effective and fulfilled.

Rather than viewing organisations as imposed structures, he suggests they should be more organic. Organisations that flourish are the ongoing creation of the people who work in them. Creating organisational structures that are rigid and imposed, synonymous with command-and-control, is way out of tune with the world we now live in.

What is clear, to me, is that it is time to:

- hand the profession back to the staff in schools;
- believe in them;
- help them build their capacity;
- foster the right conditions for effective teacher/student relationships;
- interfere less and trust more;
- accept finally that, more than any other factor, it is the teacher who will make the difference.

Michael Barber and Mona Mourshed, in their report about how the world's best education systems come out on top, state categorically that *the quality of the education system cannot exceed the quality of its teachers*.[6] Barber is unequivocal in daring teachers to be controllers of their own destiny and challenges the profession to get into its mind that it is its own job to solve the problems of the education system.[7]

But it will not be easy. Theory X thinking still simmers in questions raised in educational publications and from the floor of my conferences.

- Should the profession engage in innovation?
- Does the profession want to engage in innovation?
- Can the profession be trusted with innovation?

In his play *The Resistible Rise of Arturo Ui*, a satirical allegory of Hitler's rise to power in Nazi Germany, Brecht warns that old ideologies die hard:[8]

> *The world was almost won by such an ape!*
> *The nations put him where his kind belong.*
> *But do not rejoice too soon at your escape –*
> *The womb he crawled from is still going strong.*

What might a world in which individuals are trusted to take control of their own destiny, in which leadership is encouraged at all levels and creativity and risk-taking become the norm, actually look like?

In his fascinating book *The World is Flat*, Thomas Friedman describes ten forces, or flatteners, which have produced a global level playing field in the twenty-first century.[9] The new world will require people who have four key characteristics:

- creativity;
- flexibility;
- portability; and
- ingenuity.

Leaders of learning, like John Keating, possess these qualities and will thrive in a world of informed professional judgement.

David Jackson described such an educational world where:[10]
- outside-in solutions are replaced by inside-out;
- solutions are co-constructed on the ground by those who have to carry them out;
- solutions are context-specific because those who top-down load them often do not know what life is like in a school;

- self-generating capacity-building replaces the daily grind of responding to a seemingly endless stream of initiatives; there is a culture of optimism and a real faith in empowerment.

If we cannot pull this off, he asks, "where will the vision and thought leadership for future schools come from?"

The signs are there that leaving innovation to the schools is paying off. The move towards distributed leadership is proof positive of the new age of trust. Let us hope this concept is not confused with just another strategy for delegating or the distributing of even more responsibility and tasks to teachers. In her book about distributed leadership, Alma Harris stresses the importance of such organisational trust to organisational development and stability.[11]

The profession is mobilising itself and the rapid growth in collaborative working is giving the profession the confidence to break free of command-and-control thinking. There is safety and strength in numbers. In England, there is a growing evidence base that when schools and collaboratives of schools are empowered to lead reform they are transforming themselves. And not just through incremental change (effecting small change to current practice; swimming with the tide or beginning where they are now and edging forward). There are numerous examples that schools are swimming against the tide and radically transforming themselves, not just through major shifts in building and curriculum design, but by starting with the future and working backwards.[12]

But there are still concerns which fuel the doubters. George Otero champions such teacher-led reform but is concerned that external directives sap their resolve and drain their energy.[13] Teachers need allies and friends to provide them with the necessary time, space and support to do two crucial things:

- to develop themselves as learners and leaders;
- to enable them to develop respectful relationships with their students, their school leaders and the broader community.

In his foreword to *The National Primary Strategy* in England, Charles Clarke, the then secretary of state for education, claimed that the enjoyment children experienced from excellent teaching is the birthright of every child. I agree with him wholeheartedly, but he did not go far enough and missed a great opportunity to suggest that it is also the right of every teacher to feel supported, trusted, listened to, appreciated, developed and cared for. Put simply, using Michael Fullan's first secret of change, they need to feel loved.[14]

Fullan sees the key to success in any organisation as *loving and investing in your employees in relation to a high quality purpose*. He refers to Barber and Mourshed's report which notes that the highest performing school systems in the world valued their employees (the teachers) as much as their customers (children and parents).

He goes on to tell the cautionary tale of Tony Alvarado (chancellor of instruction) and his boss Alan Bersin (superintendent) in San Diego. Alvarado had been the highly successful leader of District 2 in New York City and was appointed in 1997 by Bersin to make similar improvements in San Diego. Using the same top-down, relentless push to improve standards that had proved so successful in New York, Alvarado met with such resistance that he was asked to leave in 2002 and Bersin himself was replaced in 2005. No one doubted the moral imperative to raise the bar on standards but neither man, Fullan claims, figured out how to love their employees as much as their customers. Carl Cohn, Bersin's replacement, wrote an article for *Education Week* entitled 'Empowering Those at the Bottom Beats Punishing Them from the Top'.

Fullan makes no apologies for the wording of his first secret of change as 'loving and investing in your employees'. Only then, I think, will teachers genuinely feel trusted and gain the confidence to truly innovate.

Such innovation, Hargreaves stresses, has to take root in the normal everyday work of teachers, alongside the very activities that are to be transformed.[15] Whatever edicts may descend from central government, it is in the day-to-day practice of professionals along corridors, across playgrounds and within the classrooms of our schools that real transformation will take place. And not all teachers will be up to the task.

Jim Collins does not fudge the issue.[16] He disagrees with those who claim that the greatest asset the leader of an organisation possesses is the people. The greatest asset the leader has, he counters, is the *right* people. The gift to be creative and imaginative must be made to every child if they are to succeed in their life and work. They will not be able to do this, Hargreaves warns, if teachers cannot learn to be innovative and creative too.

- The culture is right.
- The time is now.
- The children are waiting and it is time for the profession to step up to the plate.

Perhaps the age of the magic-weaver has started.

John Keating's creative, innovative style far from
being mistrusted and ultimately rejected, would find
itself centre stage in a culture of informed
professional judgement.

A pedagogy for justice

At the core of this innovation and all creative activity is the relationship between two human beings: the student and the teacher. The push towards greater inclusion and the implementation of such policies as *Every Child Matters* (UK) and *No Child Left Behind* (USA) has reminded the profession of its moral purpose and maybe even enabled it to rediscover its soul.[17]

Such thinking will require us to rethink the curriculum, to constantly revisit our moral purpose and to learn to love the questions as much as the answers.[18]

I agree with Professor Bart McGettrick that the purpose of education is not the curriculum but what is contained in the curriculum.[19] He sees the latter as merely a means to an end. The purposes of education, he believes, are:

- to form people of love, care and compassion;
- to develop individuals with a deep appreciation of beauty;
- to help create those who will serve others by their gifts;
- to foster an awareness of one's inner self and what it is to be a human being;
- to become someone more than we thought we could be;
- to make, foster and keep relationships..

It is, therefore, the responsibility of those who work with young people to ensure not only that the curriculum is fit for purpose but also that it is delivered by those who possess or aspire to such qualities. It is these magic-weavers who model the right attitudes and behaviour that will have a huge impact on students.

McGettrick worked from time to time with children who suffered from cerebral palsy. He was astounded by the dedication of the staff who worked with the children. They would spend six months working with just one child, hour after hour, day after day, week after week simply to enable a youngster to move her thumb from the inside to the outside of her fist. Because the teacher knows that if this young girl can achieve this, she will be able to dress, lift and feed herself. He called this social transformation or, more evocatively, *pedagogy for justice*. I call it magic-weaving.

There is a dual responsibility on government. First, to support, encourage and empower leaders in schools to get the wrong people off the bus and the right people on the bus.[20] Second to ensure that those who train the teachers of the future get it right. I humbly offer my template for their consideration.

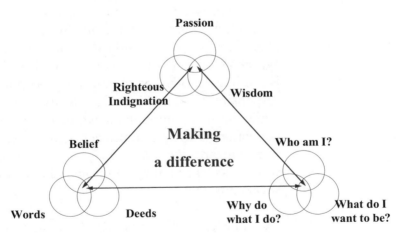

Model H: Circles of Calling (p15), Synchronicity (p18) and Reflection (p37)

Such a process would help develop individuals with passion, wisdom and a sense of righteous indignation. Reflective people, not afraid to reflect on who they are, why they live and work in the way they do and continually ponder what they might become. Human beings whose words, actions and beliefs are in synchronicity.

With such people, we will have a teaching force that will be unstoppable. A student once said to me, "The future is important to me, it's where I intend to spend the rest of my life." Supported by such people, his future will be in safe hands.

In an age when demographics still equals destiny Bob Barr and Bill Parrett are right when they describe education as the ultimate civil right. If every child is to matter and none be left behind, the next decade will be crucial. Teachers able to inform, motivate and inspire young people will be able to use learning to break, once and for all, the link between where you are born and how well you do.

In the 1994 movie *The Shawshank Redemption*, Andy Dufresne (Tim Robbins) is wrongly sentenced to two life sentences. In the prison he strikes up a close friendship with Red (Morgan Freeman). Warden Norton (Bob Gunton) recognises that Andy is not like the other prisoners and gives him the responsibility of looking after his office. One day, while thumbing through the warden's record collection, Dufresne comes across the *Letter Duet* from Mozart's *Le Nozze di Figaro* and, much to the warden's chagrin, plays it through the prison's speaker system.

Red, in Morgan Freeman's mellifluous voice, describes the effect it had:

> *I have no idea to this day what those two Italian ladies were singing about. Truth is I don't want to know. I tell you those two voices soared, higher and farther than anyone in a*

place like this dares to dream. It was as if
some beautiful bird had flown into our drab
little cage and made those walls dissolve away.

That last sentence captures perfectly, I think, the role
of the magic-weaver:

- The ability to win from young people their
  permission to take them to places where they
  cannot go alone.
- To see beyond the sometimes ugly reality of
  their drab little cage.
- To be the keeper of their dreams.
- To know where they are, yet always see what
  they could be.

Joshua Bell is one of the world's most gifted
violinists and played the soundtrack in the 1998
movie *The Red Violin*. John Corigliano won an
Oscar for Best Original Dramatic Score. Receiving
his award, he gave the credit to Bell who, he said,
played like a god. On January 9, 2007, Bell filled
Boston's Symphony Hall with an average ticket cost
of $100.

In Washington, three days later, encouraged by a
Washington Post reporter and dressed in jeans and a
baseball cap, he took his 18th century Stradivarius,
worth in the region of $3.5 million, down to the
Metro station. He played for 43 minutes as 1,097
people passed by. His playing grossed $32.17
donated by 27 people, most of whom did not stop to
listen.

Michael Keaney, Director of the Long Island School
Leadership Centre, used this story in a letter to his
colleagues. He wondered how much richness do we
pass each day and fail to notice because we are too

busy, too driven, and too blind. I wonder how many Joshua Bells we pass on the school corridor each day and just don't notice. Keaney concluded:

This year, I have heard so many stories of good people in education who made a difference in someone's life because they stopped and saw something no-one else did. I also learned first hand how incredibly supportive our local education community is when someone is hurting and needs help. I'll never forget those people who took the time to care.

Bart McGettrick once explained how in 1451, the year before the birth of Christopher Columbus, Glasgow University was established by Pope Nicholas V. The papal bull, among other things, stated that the purpose of the university was 'to help and raise to distinction those born in the lowest of places'. Maybe social inclusion is not such a new idea. He went on to describe education as the profession of hope in the service of others.

I often wonder why doctors take the Hippocratic oath, soldiers have the Oath of Enlistment and yet there is no oath for those who are entrusted with the futures of our young? So, with the help of Bart McGettrick, here goes:

I do solemnly swear that I will, to the best of my ability, work with the young to help:

- *form people of love, care and compassion who have a deep appreciation of beauty*
- *develop people who serve others by their gifts*
- *raise people to distinction*

So help me God.

After the great fire of London in 1666, although he wanted to be an astronomer and philosopher, Christopher Wren was commissioned to build St Paul's Cathedral. In 1671 he visited the site and observed three brick layers. One was crouched down, the second was half-standing, while the third was working feverishly.

"What are you doing?" Wren asked the men.

"Laying bricks," the first replied.

"Making a living," answered the second.

The third paused from his labour and explained that he was helping to build a cathedral and that one day people would come to pray to God in the cathedral he had helped to build.

I challenge you to remember your magic-weavers. I challenge you, too, to find out where they are and say thank you. For they were not just laying bricks, nor earning money. They were helping you to build your cathedral.

A threshold adventure like no other.

The magic-weaving business.

References and notes for Chapter 6

[1] The definition of culture attributed to Gerard Egan. See: Egan, Gerard (1994), *Working the Shadow Side: A guide to positive behind-the-scenes management.* San Francisco, CA: Jossey-Bass.

[2] Barber, Michael (2002), *From Good to Great: Large-scale Reform in England.* Paper presented to Futures of Education conference, April 23, Universitat Zurich. New Jersey: Prentice Hall. Sir Michael Barber worked at the centre of government education policy during the first term of Tony Blair's government from 1997 to 2001. He went on to head up the Prime Minister's Delivery Unit at 10 Downing Street. In 2005 he joined the consulting firm McKinsey.

[3] McGregor, Douglas (1960), *The Human Side of Enterprise.* New York: McGraw-Hill.

[4] Flaherty, James (2005), *Coaching: Evoking excellence in others (2nd edition).* Burlington, MA: Elsevier Butterworth-Heinemann.

[5] Andrew Fraser visited Ontario, England, Scotland and Germany during his Winston Churchill Memorial Trust Fellowship from Australia. His comments are independent and a professional reflection on the state of the teaching profession in England. A copy of his Fellowship report may be accessed through this link:
www.churchilltrust.encode.net.au/res/File/Fellow_Reports/Fraser%20Andrew%202005.pdf

[6] Barber, Michael and Mourshed, Mona (2007), *How the World's Best Performing Systems Come Out on Top.* New York: McKinsey. The report is available via this link:
www.mckinsey.com/clientservice/socialsector/resources/pdf/Worlds_School_systems_final.pdf

[7] See The Guardian, Education section, 23 May 2006, in an article titled *The Risk-Takers*.

[8] Brecht, Berthold (1941), *The Resistible Rise of Arturi Uri.*

[9] Friedman, Thomas L. (2006), *The World is Flat: A Brief History of the Twenty-first Century (2nd edition).* London: Penguin Books.

[10] Jackson, David (2003), *Networked learning communities and their contribution to sustainable school improvement: A UK perspective.* Presentation to Victorian Association of Secondary School Principals Conference. David Jackson was director of the Network Learning Group at the National College for School Leadership (England).

[11] Harris, Alma (2008), *Distributed Leadership in Schools: Developing the Leaders of Tomorrow.* London: Routledge and Falmer Press. Alma Harris is pro-director for leadership at the Institute of Education, University of London and director of the London Centre for Leadership in Learning.

[12] Hannon, Valerie (2007), *'Next Practice' in Education: a disciplined approach to innovation.* London: Innovations Unit. This pamphlet can be obtained through this weblink: www.innovation-unit.co.uk/about-us/publications/next-practice-in-education.html

[13] Otero, George (2003), *Conversations for school improvement: the value of relational learning.* Camberwell, Victoria: Australian Council for Educational Research, APC Monographs. Dr. George Otero is Director of the Center of Relational Learning, Santa Fe, New Mexico, USA.

[14] Fullan, Michael (2008), *The Six Secrets of Change: What the Best Leaders Do to Help Their Organisations Survive and Thrive.* San Francisco, CA: Jossey-Bass.

[15] Hargreaves, Andy and Shirley, Dennis (2009), *The Fourth Way: The Inspiring Future for Educational Change.* Thousand Oaks, CA: Corwin Press.

[16] Collins, Jim (2001), *Good to Great.* New York: HarperCollins.

[17] *Every Child Matters* is the title of a shared programme of change to improve outcomes for all children and young people in England. You may explore the different strands of the programme at this website: www.dcsf.gov.uk/everychildmatters/.
The *No Child Left Behind* (NCLB) Act in 2002 introduced a standards-based reform program across the United States to improve students' test scores. You can read the Act at this link: www.ed.gov/policy/elsec/leg/esea02/index.html

[18] Fullan, Michael (2001), *Leading in a Culture of Change.* San Francisco, CA: Jossey-Bass.

[19] From Bart McGettrick's inaugural lecture, *Christian Education and Contemporary Culture* at Liverpool Hope University, 30 January 2008.

[20] According to Collins (see reference [16]).

·

Acknowledgements

The author is grateful to the following:

The National Commission on Teaching and America's Future for permission to include the text excerpt on page 2 from *What Matters Most: Teaching for America's Future*. New York: NCTAF. Published in 1996.

Andy Hargreaves for permission to include the text excerpt on page 20 from *The Long and Short of Educational Change* previously published in *Education Canada* 2007.

Michael Fullan for permission to include the text excerpt on page 71 from *Leadership for the 21st Century* previously published in *Education Leadership* 1998.

Alistair Smith for permission to include the text excerpt on page 115 from *Help Your Child to Succeed: The Essential Guide for Parents*. Stafford: Network Educational Press. Published in 2002.

Ian Gilbert for permission to include the text excerpt on page 130 from *The Little Book of Thunks: 260 questions to make your brain go ouch!* Published in 2008.

Alan Boyle who kept me believing this book was possible and whose determination, skill and sweat made it happen.

INDEX

Tice, L., 62, 76, 82, 97